THE BRIDGE OVER THE RIVER KWAI
was built in less than two m_____ by the exhausted prisoners.

But the a_____
changed th_____

D1203354

THROUGH THE VALLEY OF THE KWAI

"THE TRUE STORY OF THE DRAMA of the Kwai Valley. Of far greater impact than the film."
—*The Jerusalem Post*

"AS READABLE AS A NOVEL. Does much of what Bonhoeffer does in *The Cost of Discipleship."* —*Southwestern Journal of Theology*

"A STRONG AFFIRMATION OF HUMAN DIGNITY." —*Book-of-the-Month Club News*

"GRIPPING—one of the great stories of faith that developed in the crucible of wartime affliction."
—*Eternity*

"THE PICTURES WILL LIVE in the memory of every reader." —*Journal of Pastoral Care*

"A THRILLING SPIRITUAL ODYSSEY."
—*Chaplain*

HARPER JUBILEE BOOKS

THROUGH the VALLEY of THE KWAI

Ernest Gordon

Harper & Row, Publishers
New York, Evanston, San Francisco, London

FIRST HARPER & ROW JUBILEE EDITION PUBLISHED IN 1975.

LIBRARY OF CONGRESS CATALOG CARD NUMBER: 62-11127

ISBN: 0-06-063353-0

75 76 77 78 79 10 9 8 7 6 5 4 3 2 1

At the special request of my children, Gillian Margaret and Alastair James, this book is dedicated to those who were my comrades in the prison camps of the Railroad of Death

contents

THROUGH

the

VALLEY

of

THE KWAI

And an highway shall be there, and a way, and it shall be called The way of holiness; the unclean shall not pass over it; but it shall be for those: the wayfaring men, though fools, shall not err therein.

Isaiah 35:8

CHAPTER 1

The Death House

I WAS DREAMING, AND I WAS HAPPY WITH MY dreams. Within myself I heard the raucous cry of sea gulls circling above the fishing boats as the fishermen sorted their catch. I felt the touch of a salt-laden wind upon my face; I smelled the clean freshness of old-fashioned carbolic soap; I tasted the sweet bitterness of heavy Scottish ale.

I sensed the many things that were calling me to life. Most happily, in my dreams, I was appreciating the cozy luxury of freshly-ironed sheets on my bed at home, and the friendly flicker of warm shadows my bedroom fire cast upon the wall.

In the bewildering no-man's land between the *was* and the *is* the pictures began to fade; the comfort departed; the crisp, clean smells of wholesomeness were overpowered. My waking senses, struggling up reluctantly from their pleasing rest, experienced anew the smells of my existence as a prisoner of war of the Japanese in the jungles of Thailand. These were the corrupt smells of dying things—of dying flesh, of dying men.

Turning my head in the direction of sounds that distracted me, I saw a small light lurching and staggering as if carried over uneven ground. I heard strained breathing and the irregular thud of bare feet on bare earth. Two British medical orderlies reached my end of the Death House with a body on a stretcher swaying between them in unsteady rhythm.

1

"Here you are, chum," said the first orderly, as they dropped their load upon the ground. "We've brought another one to keep you company."

The yellow glow of the makeshift lamp gave enough light for me to see my comrades of the night. They were ten dead men dressed in their shrouds of straw rice sacks. It was hard to tell that they were corpses. They might have been bags of old rags or old bones. The uncertain light and the position from which I was looking at them—the ground—made them seem longer and heavier and more important than they were. Even if they had been more clearly discernible as bodies —as forms emptied of their humanity—I would not have minded. Corpses were as common among us as empty bellies.

I was lying in the morgue end of the Death House. Being on slightly higher and therefore less muddy terrain, this end was the most desirable section of the long, slummy bamboo hut which was supposed to be a hospital but had long since given up any pretense of being a place to shelter the sick. It was a place where men came to die.

"I hope no more shuffle off tonight," I whispered.

"Don't worry," said the orderly, "this one's probably the last. There are two R.C.'s ready to go; but like as not they'll hang on till morning. The priest gave them absolution last night, so they're all right. You know what they call that priest?"

I shook my head.

"The Angel of Death. Every time they see him come in, the R.C.'s wonder which of 'em is due to go. Some of the chaps don't mind knowing, but some are still too sensitive.

" 'Nothing much you can do about it,' I says to 'em. 'He has his job to do and I daresay he doesn't like it any better than anyone else.' Cor, I bet he was never kept half so busy in Blighty. If he was to be paid a quid for every one he sees off, he'd be a bleeding millionaire."

The orderlies rolled the corpse onto the ground and began fitting it with two rice sacks.

"How old was he?" I asked.

"Oh, about twenty-one," the first orderly replied. "He was in the Service Corps with the Eighteenth Division. Only came into Chungkai about five days ago."

They went about their task like old hands, pulling one sack over the head and the other over the feet. While they were pulling up the lower sack the left hand flopped over on the ground. As it lay there, uselessly, hopelessly, it seemed the most significantly dead thing about the body. Queer, how dead it looked. It was good for nothing. The hand could work no more, nor be raised in protest, nor point to something worthy of attention, nor touch another gently. Its stillness seemed to shout, "See, I'm dead!"

The hand was stuffed into the sack, both sacks were tied together with pieces of atap grass, and the body was stacked along with others about two feet from where I was lying.

"Might as well have a rest," said the first orderly.

"It's been a long night," observed his mate. They sat down beside me.

"The only ambition I have," the first one said after a bit, "is to die of old age. Cor, it would be nice to have a son or two. Watch them grow up under your eyes; and then when you've had your life, see that they come round to keep you company. It would be a bit of all right, it would."

He sighed.

"All this here death is so useless because it's at the wrong time," he continued. "It's death for nothing. The time's been mucked up. Everything is mucked up here. A man should have a bit of dignity for himself, even in death. But that's what we haven't got."

The orderlies picked up the stretcher, ready once more to play their part as hosts in the House of the Dead.

They made their way back down the hut, taking their lamp with them, leaving me in darkness. I was now so thoroughly awake that I couldn't go back to sleep. I resented this, for sleep was the most precious thing I could experience. It wasn't that I minded lying on the ground; my body had practically no feeling left in it. Since nature had anesthetized it, why couldn't it have done the same with my mind and granted me peace?

I could not say as Odysseus did, "Be strong my heart: ere now worse fate was thine"—it was hard to imagine a worse fate. However, I could say, as Achilles did to Odysseus in Hades, "Don't say a word in favor of death; rather would I be a serving man in a pauper's home and be above ground than be a king of kings among the dead."

To all intents the advantage still was mine. I was alive. I could think. I existed.

The dawn came suddenly and harshly, bringing with it bright light, sharp shadows, and stifling heat. The hut looked more like a Death House than ever—filthy, squalid, and decayed.

Through the gaps in the atap walls I could see open latrines, and beyond them bamboos touching bamboos in an endless mass that reached out for a thousand miles to where freedom lay—and also reached in to hold us fast.

Yes, I knew where I was; I was in a prison camp by the River Kwai. I knew who I was; I was a company commander in the 93rd Highlanders. And yet I wasn't. I was a prisoner of war, a man lying with the dead, waiting for them to be carried away that I might have more room.

Fingering my black beard, I wondered why I had to end up in such a place. What a contrast this was to the way my ill-starred odyssey had begun—a beginning associated in my mind with summer in a civilized, or comparatively civilized, world.

It was a good summer, that summer of 1939. I had hurried from the University of St. Andrews to my home on the Firth of Clyde in time to take part in an ocean race to the south of Ireland and back on the old Clyde *Forty Vagrant*.

The summer had a stormy beginning, for a northeaster dispersed the fleet on the homeward leg and we had to limp into Dublin for repairs.

But from then on, life was a series of gay regattas and long, happy cruises. Skies were blue, winds fair and warm. The Firth was saturated with beauty. Each day, each event, each incident seemed better than the one before. I had very little money, but I lived like a millionaire on what small skill I had as a yachtsman.

In July, I skippered a yacht on a cruise up the Scottish west coast, seeking harbor at night in lochs protected by hills ancient with wisdom and offering a rare serenity to those ready to receive it.

That cruise over, I sailed from Sandbank to Cowes in my favorite yacht, the *Dione*. It was a "couthy" sail, the whole seven hundred miles of it. My crewmates had a hearty lust for life. The four of us were on a spree, conscious perhaps that we had to make the most of all that was clean and dignified. Although I sailed continuously, there was always time for a girl in most ports. The more interesting the girl, the more favored the port.

There was, however, an ominous undertone. Perhaps my foreboding was due to a feeling that I was living on borrowed time. I'd had a spell of duty in the Royal Air Force, terminating in an accident that left me with a fractured skull and spine. While recovering I sensed that the drums of war were already sounding. I decided that before going to battle I would spend time at the university to read history and philosophy more for my own enjoyment than for anything else.

My disablement had granted me a pleasant respite from

the profession of arms. The future was so uncertain that I did not worry much about preparing for any other career. In my own fashion I was bent on savoring the delight of living. Today was mine, tomorrow could wait.

Fair winds and noble yachts, good companions and bonnie lassies, happy times and laughing days, seldom last as long as we would like. So busy was I in pursuit of my favorite sport that I paid no attention to what was happening on the international scene.

On August 23, Germany signed a nonaggression pact with Russia while I was taking part in an inter-varsity regatta. I did not learn this until I returned to my lodgings in Clynder at the close of the day's racing to find a telegram for me lying on the hall table. It was from my parents, telling me that my brother had been called up in the Royal Engineers and suggesting that it was time I returned home. The halcyon days were over. A long, fearsome struggle confronted us all.

I had made up my mind I would not pass it "flying a desk." If I couldn't fight in the air I would fight on the ground. Back home, I picked up the telephone and called the secretary of our local Territorial Association in Dunoon to inquire if there were any vacancies for commissions in the Argyll and Sutherland Highlanders. I was told there were and if I rushed over I could have one fairly soon.

I was posted first to one of the Territorial Battalions and then, after a month or so, to the Second Battalion—the 93rd Highlanders.

This battalion originated during the Napoleonic Wars when the Duke of Sutherland was urged to raise a regiment in his own county in the northeast corner of Scotland. Those he sought to recruit were so independent that at first they refused to accept the king's shilling. They came around eventually when they were allowed to serve under fellow highlanders rather than English officers and to take their own kirk to war

with them as part of the regiment. After the battle of Balacla ,
the battalion became known as the "Thin Red Line" because
it had halted the Russian cavalry charge. In the reign of Queen
Victoria it was united with the 91st or Argyllshire Highlanders to form the Argyll and Sutherland Highlanders. The
93rd made up the Second Battalion. At the outbreak of World
War I the regiment was the first to land in France and the
first to see action.

Although we were a highland regiment, most of our officers
came either from south of the Highland Fault Line or south
of the border. Our Jocks (G.I.'s) came from the industrial
belt stretching between the Forth and Clyde Rivers: from
Edinburgh, Falkirk, Motherwell, Hamilton, Clydebank,
Greenock, Gourock, Port-Glasgow, and Stirling.

They were in the army for a variety of reasons: because
soldiering was in their blood, tales of martial glory having
been imbibed with their mother's milk; because the glamor of a
soldier's uniform offered a cheerful contrast to the squalor
of the slums; because it provided a means to stay alive; or
because they were running away from something.

After I was mobilized I visited St. Andrews to fetch some
books and see friends. I went straight to the bar of the Im-
perial Hotel, a popular students' haunt, to show off my fine
new uniform with its bright Glengarry bonnet, its badger's
head sporran, and green-and-blue box-pleated kilt. The bar
was almost empty except for a traveling salesman and a fellow
student of pronounced Marxist views. The student, lounging
against the bar, surveyed me.

"What the hell are you doing in that uniform? Don't you
know it will all be over by Christmas? You're just wasting
your own time and the taxpayers' money."

His remark shocked me. But it was to take many shocks to
shake us from our complacent belief that all would soon be
back to normal.

, 1939, I was given a week's embarkation
last in what was to be a long war. This was
experience. It rained all the time. I went around
but those I knew had already scattered. I had
ceive a hero's farewell from my girl friends. But
the, had gone to serve king and country in one or another
of the services. I slept for the last time in the comfort of my
own bed, bade a sad farewell to my parents, my sister Grace
and my brother Pete, and caught the train for regimental
headquarters at Stirling Castle.

To the north of Glasgow, halfway between the Rivers Clyde
and Forth, the castle stands with its turrets thrust aggressively
skyward, as though conscious of its role as sentinel on the
route to the highlands.

On a misty gray Saturday afternoon several weeks later,
I paraded on the square with a small detachment of first-
line reinforcements. At the far end stood a contingent of
national service men newly arrived and still wearing their
civilian clothes. They eyed us with awe, conscious of the fact
that we were soldiers and on our way to war. Among them, I
recognized Gordon Shiach, a friend of my boyhood from
Dunoon. We had no chance to speak. I wondered if I would
ever see him again.

The orderly sergeant of the day took the roll call of my
men, and handed them over to me as "all present and correct."
Hurriedly, I inspected them and gave the order to slope arms.
Then, with a "right turn" and a "quick march" we were off.
The sentry at the main gate came to attention, and presented
arms in salute as we marched from that high, stark fastness.

There is only one way out of Stirling Castle and that is
down. Downhill we marched, down the steep brae, past the
Castle Inn where the "other ranks" drank their beer, down
past the Red Lion where the officers sipped their scotch, down
the cobbled main street that led to the railroad station.

The streets of Stirling looked much the same as on any other Saturday. Housewives dragged reluctant husbands along or left them standing as they paused to gossip while their men thought wistfully of the football games they might have been following on the wireless. No trumpet blew; there were no hurrahs; no one cried; we passed unnoticed on our way to war. The day of the soldier had not yet arrived.

Downward our way continued—all the way down the world: down through England, down through France by stages; down through the Red Sea and the Indian Ocean by troopship; down through the dripping jungle of Malaya on foot; down through the mud and the blood in the heartbreaking retreat to the last stand in Singapore; down, until all that was left of our thousand-strong battalion was a battered remnant of one hundred and twenty.

We had reached the end of the Malayan mainland. A sturdy Causeway, supporting a railway and a double road, connected the mainland with the Island of Singapore. Under cover of darkness, thirty thousand men crossed over on January 31, 1942, without a single casualty.

In keeping with the regimental tradition, the Argylls were the last to cross the Causeway. Also in line with our tradition, Colonel Ian Stewart, the battalion commanding officer, his batman, and I, as rear company commander, were the last ones of our battalion.

We sauntered across as though on exercise, while our two surviving pipers played "Highland Laddie," the regimental march. As we set foot on the mainland we heard a mighty bang and saw a great cloud of dust and flying rubble. The Causeway had been blown, sealing in the inhabitants along with the island's defenders. There was now no place to go.

With the rest of the garrison, our remnant fought on until, of the remaining one hundred and twenty of our battalion, only thirty were left; until, on February 15, the British defending forces ran out of ammunition, drinking water—and hope.

And even after that, my own way continued on down, down across the Straits by commandeered ferry to Sumatra, where my journey came to a halt in a coastal city called Padang.

CHAPTER 2

Soldiers at Sea

THE LAST BRITISH WARSHIP TAKING OFF refugees had sailed from Padang a few days before I got there. The whole of Sumatra was about to fall. I was on my own, without command, without instructions. I realized I'd better be planning how I could get away. I'd have to do it soon if I was going to do it at all, for the enemy was already closing in on the city. Australia, India, and Ceylon were the nearest countries free of Japanese domination. But they were all a considerable distance away.

I was walking down the main street one morning, pondering ways and means, when a familiar voice hailed me. Behind me was a British colonel of the India Army Service Corps whom I recognized at once. He was one of those I had passed along from Singapore via the escape route.

"I thought you'd be on your way to India by this time," I said as we shook hands, "on board one of those cruisers that picked up the last loads."

He shrugged fatalistically.

"Not my luck. I followed your example and stayed to organize a transit camp a little upriver from you. I got into Padang two days before you did. Then I heard you had arrived and I've been hunting for you ever since. May I have a word with you?"

"Certainly," I said, curious to know what he had on his mind.

He led the way to a coffeehouse which had a few iron tables set out under a canopy. Two Malays in black sunkas (brimless caps), and white bajus (open-necked shirts), were paying their chits and getting up to leave.

The waiter brought us our coffee. When he had moved away, the colonel said to me in a matter-of-fact voice,

"I'm forming an official escape party. I wonder if you'd care to join?"

I stared at him dumfounded.

"Of course I would! What's the plan?"

He leaned closer across the table.

"One of the last messages we received from General Wavell's H.Q. was to the effect that an attempt to escape should be made by a group of officers—if no help arrives. It appears most unlikely that any help will get through to us before the Japs take over."

I nodded. "I'm afraid that seems obvious—worse luck."

"As senior officer, it is my responsibility to see that the order is carried through. I have the names of all British officers who have come to Sumatra as well as the last known of the Army in Singapore before its capture."

"Good," I said, trying to curb my impatience. "What do you have in mind?"

"I've been in touch with the Netherlands Government people in Padang. They say they do not want to do anything official—if the Japs found out they would be punished."

The colonel was determined to take his time in unfolding the plot.

"Unofficially, however, they have given me a sum of money, saying that it is none of their business what I do with it. They have also loaned me two cars to be returned when I've finished with them—and no questions asked."

Then, with maddening deliberation, he continued,

"A hundred miles north there's a fishing village called

Sasok. From what I gather there's a possibility that we may be able to buy a sailing boat."

It sounded too good to be true. I must have looked incredulous.

"Well, not a proper sailing boat," he said, "not quite what you're used to at the Royal Singapore Yacht Club. But she would have sail—and she would float. The southwest monsoon is due to break in May. With a bit of luck we may benefit from its winds a little earlier than that and make Ceylon quite comfortably."

"Oh, I should think so," I said. "Ceylon can't be more than twelve hundred miles."

The colonel frowned. "But it won't be all that easy—not with the Jap Navy and their Air Force in command of the Indian Ocean."

"Who all are going?" I asked.

"I've worked out a list of nine. You may know some of them. There are three navy types: Crawley—remember him? He sailed up to H.Q. in Tambilihan in a junk. And two from the Malay Volunteer Force. Then there's a major from the Sappers, and a captain from the Signals. Including myself —and you—we'll make ten altogether."

"Could you include two more?" I asked. "I'd like Rigden and MacLaren to come along. They were with me on the escape boat."

The colonel shook his head.

"Sorry, old boy. I'm afraid it isn't possible."

I felt that I was letting my friends down. He continued,

"Rigden has been assigned as dockmaster, you know, in case a warship should come in. And MacLaren has been put in charge of the troops as sergeant major."

"Are you sure we can't change that?" I pleaded.

"Absolutely. We've got to get cracking. Besides, we'd be doing them no great favor. This will be a risky business. If we're caught, we're likely to be executed."

This eased my conscience somewhat.

"When do we leave for Sasok?"

"At dawn, day after tomorrow."

"Anything I can do in the meantime?"

"Don't think so, thank you. The Malayan Reserve officers have been given the job of picking up as many tins of food as they can find. The New Zealand naval officer is out hunting up navigational instruments and a book of nautical tables. The Sapper is putting together a first-aid box—and I think that's about it."

He seemed to be ticking everything off in his mind. Then he said,

"Oh, tell you what. You might invest in some cigarettes. They'd come in handy for barter."

"Now, what about clothing?"

"Take what you have. I expect it isn't much."

I smiled.

"Only what I have on—plus a spare pair of shorts, a shirt, my toothbrush and shaving gear."

"Oh, you might see if you can pick up some native clothing. It would come in handy if we have to pass ourselves off as Malay fishermen," he added.

"What about weapons?" I asked, warming to the prospect of the adventure. "I happen to know where I can pick up some submachine guns."

The colonel frowned.

"No, that won't be necessary. As a matter of fact, it wouldn't be such a good idea. Chances are we'll be dealing with natives and it might put the wind up if they saw us armed to the teeth. We'll take our sidearms. That's all we'll need."

The colonel drained the last drop of coffee from his cup, lighted a cigarette, and lounged back comfortably in his chair. He was ready for chitchat.

"Tell me, how did you get away from Singapore?"

"Someone at Command conceived the brilliant idea of running a ferry service between Malaya and Singapore to bring in supplies. I was to be in charge."

"Did it ever begin operation?"

"No, it was nothing more than an idea—based on the assumption that Singapore would hold out indefinitely."

"Quite an assumption, wasn't it? I suppose some of the staff may have believed it."

"Perhaps. The staff seemed capable of believing anything as far as I could see." I said this with a typical infantry officer's disdain of staff wallahs.

"What happened?"

"As you know, everything seemed to be in a state of utter confusion. On Friday morning—that was the Black Friday of February 13—I was ordered to go to one of the islands off Changi that was garrisoned by the Second Dogras. I was to take them on ferry boats and land them behind the Jap lines on the west sector of Singapore Island."

"By that time the decision was about three days too late, was it not?"

"Yes it was. When I reached the Dogras' H.Q. I learned that the whole deal was off. First thing next morning I went down to the jetty to see what I could see. There I discovered a ferry boat that had arrived the night before. It was commanded by Sergeant Major MacLaren. He didn't know quite what to do, so he was glad to see me turn up in the hope that I did. I didn't. But I sent a signal to Command H.Q., telling them I was on my way in the ferry. H.Q. replied that I was to proceed on my own. We made it back to Keppel Harbor. As we were entering, a battery shelled us. We moved out into the Straits and lay there till Sunday.

"All that day we kept picking up boatloads of escapees. Each had a different story to tell. Around midnight we came across four men in a canoe. From them we learned that the show was over—had been over since eight thirty that evening."

"That's about the time the C.O. sent his last message," mused the colonel. " 'Owing to losses from enemy action—water, petrol, food, and ammunition practically finished. Unable therefore to continue to fight any longer.' It was the sign-off. Too bad I hadn't bumped into you then. I might have had a more comfortable trip."

I laughed.

"I'm not so sure about that. I had no charts and I didn't know where the mine fields were. But we got the ferry through and sailed up the Indragiri to Rengat. There we found everything in a bonnie mess. I had picked up Tom Rigden on the way. When we heard about the nurses, women, and children who were left behind in the islands, we wanted to stay and run an escape service for the ones who were stranded after the Jap attacks on the last convoy from Singapore."

"That was a rough deal, wasn't it? I understand the whole convoy was sunk."

"Yes, I guess so. We picked up quite a few of the survivors. The nurses put up a terrific show."

"Was there anyone at Rengat trying to organize things?"

"Oh, yes, there was a major in the special branch of Intelligence who was doing his best to straighten things out. It was he who suggested that I go back to Tambilihan and run things from there. As a matter of fact, he gave me this paper. He had the idea that we could get co-operation from the Dutch and put together some kind of resistance movement."

I reached in my hip pocket for my wallet, drew out a slip, and read from it:

" 'This is to say that Captain Ernest Gordon of the Argyll and Sutherland Highlanders is empowered to act on behalf of His Majesty's Government. Any assistance given to him in the form of money, arms, or equipment will be paid for at a later date. All bills incurred by him as military representative in Sumatra will be honored.' "

A gleam lighted up the colonel's eyes.

"Keep that!" he exclaimed. "It may prove useful."

I folded the chit carefully, returning it to my wallet. It did not occur to me then that far from proving useful, it might put my life in jeopardy.

The colonel pushed back his chair, and looked at his watch.

"About time I moved along," he said. "I'm meeting the British Acting Vice-Consul at noon."

He lowered his voice.

"Morning after next. Be outside the government school by five o'clock. No later. Good-by."

The first suggestion of dawn was paling the sky behind the palm trees as shadowy figures began to materialize in the schoolyard. Introductions were brief. The borrowed cars were packed and ready. With a minimum of fuss and delay we took our places.

The soft pastel colors of the buildings around us were beginning to show as the wheels crunched on the gravel of the driveway and we set off, heading north for Sasok.

"It's a long haul to freedom," I thought to myself, listening to the music of the wheels on the road. "But at least we're on our way."

At Fort De Kock we found the headquarters of the Dutch forces. The officers informed us that the Japanese were advancing rapidly and that to proceed farther would mean certain capture. We chose to risk it.

When we passed their forward positions, we began to appreciate the wisdom of their counsel. We crossed a bridge. A few moments later we heard a muffled *boom*. It had just been blown. At the first opportunity we turned off the main highway onto a single-track side road which wound and twisted up into the hills. We were in the nick of time. From the top of the first rise we saw the dust of a Japanese column rising from the road we had just left.

The mountain track in itself was breathtaking, leading up and down steep hills, across roaring torrents on shaky bridges, and through dark cavernous jungle until we left the hills behind and entered the coastal area. Before long we came upon a fair-sized village where the Dutch controller, or administrator, had his headquarters. He received us warmly, handed us a letter to his assistant at Sasok, and sold us a case of beer.

In the late afternoon we reached the village, located at the mouth of a river. We were pleased to see two fairly seaworthy-looking craft of a Malay type called prahus tied up along the bank. With the assistant controller's help we opened negotiations at once and finally bought one for a price of two thousand guilders. Judging by the expressions of the onlookers, the Malays had by far the better of it.

The prahu of our choice was named the *Setia Berganti*. She was about fifty feet over all and rather broad in the beam. Her deckhouse, thatched and canted like the roof of a hut, ran almost the length of the ship, leaving only a short deck space fore and aft. Her unusually long bowsprit, lending a rakish air, was her only saving grace. Her hull, however, appeared to be sound and her bottom was copper-sheathed. She was not exactly a thing of grace and beauty, but she was our Argus of fortune.

"Puts you in mind of Noah's Ark, doesn't it?"

A well-set-up man, fair of complexion and easy in manner, was standing at my side, also looking the prahu over. He was Edward Hooper, former harbor master of Singapore and member of the Royal Malayan Naval Reserve, who was to be our skipper. In his spotless white naval shorts and shirt, his white knee-length stockings and white shoes, he was the picture of smartness and efficiency. He seemed to have little in common with the dowdy craft.

The skipper identified a small kiosk on the portside of the foredeck as the wood-burning galley, and a big box suspended overside from the starboard shrouds as the combined bathhouse and head. The vessel had one drawback as far as comfort was concerned—she had no sleeping quarters. Her Malay crews, so Hooper said, slept on the copra cargoes. I looked at her rig.

"Queer setup," I noted. "It's a ketch, but I don't like the way the main boom runs abaft the mizzen. We'll need to top it up every time we go about. Heaven help us if we ever have an accidental jibe."

"Wouldn't be a good thing to have happen," the skipper mused. "Perhaps we'd best have a closer look at the sails."

We walked up the short gangplank and went aboard. He fingered a fold of sail.

"Not much better than butter muslin."

"A bit on the gossamer side," I agreed. "Think we'll ever make Ceylon with those?"

"Touch and go," the skipper replied. "Perhaps you'd better visit the shops and lay in a few bolts of cloth in case we have to make repairs."

By the time I returned with some bolts of heavy cotton cloth it was getting dark. The village headman offered to let us spend the night in the one-room school and we gladly accepted. Excited as we were at the prospect of escape we had difficulty in settling ourselves for the night. We kept up a running crossfire of conversation.

"Golly, these floors are hard," moaned Limey, the British naval officer who was to be our cook. He had been hurt in the shoulder by a fragment of high explosive in the naval battle on Black Friday and was thrashing about trying to make himself comfortable.

"Not so hard as the floors in a Jap prison," retorted Anzac, the New Zealand type. "I'll take these any time. We're still free and we've a shot at a getaway. I wonder how those poor blighters in Singapore are making out?"

"Hard to tell, Anzac," the colonel sighed. "There's been no word. One thing you can be sure of, though . . . they're having no picnic."

"You're so right," the skipper put in. "If we set sail as quickly as possible we'll never find out what being a prisoner of war is like."

"And keep going at all costs," said Limey. "It's me for the girls and the gay times in Ceylon. I'm sure to know some girls there. I know girls everywhere."

"Stow the girls," the colonel growled. "We've a hard job tomorrow. We need our sleep."

At dawn we were awakened by a babble of voices. Natives, who had come at the headman's behest, were streaming by our quarters, loaded down with foodstuffs. Soon the school-yard took on the appearance of a market, with baskets of pineapples, limes, eggs, yams, pawpaws, pomelos, dried fish, dried prawns, and bananas spread out over the ground.

We left Limey in charge of the victualing and went to carry out our assigned tasks. All that day we worked like beavers, loading ballast, stores, and water, overhauling the rigging and splicing rope. It was good to be busy again.

Our water supply was stored in six former oil drums of fifty-five gallons capacity each, and ninety four-gallon erstwhile gasoline cans, giving us a total of six hundred and ninety gallons. We estimated this would afford us an ample supply for thirty days plus, long enough to reach Ceylon, with due allowance for evaporation and spoilage, for the gasoline cans were open at the top.

Provisions appeared more than adequate. We had brought

aboard two baskets of canned goods and two large sacks of rice. We were taking along all the green fruit Limey had been able to buy, and had hard-boiled a quantity of duck eggs. We also had an emergency reserve of both food and liquid in the form of green coconuts. We stowed all our supplies in the hold and covered them with split bamboo to serve as our only sleeping deck.

Toward evening we had brought order out of confusion and it was with a grateful sigh that we saw the last of our supplies safely aboard the prahu.

The village headman announced that he was giving us a farewell party. A throng of laughing children escorted us back to the village center.

Our hearts warmed toward the headman when we saw all the pains he had taken in our behalf. Mountains of fried chicken, rice, and delectable fruits awaited us. We ate our fill, knowing that it would be a long time before we again enjoyed such a meal. In pantomime and with gestures, they bade us farewell. One toothless old man waved his hands up and down and blew lustily with his mouth. We knew he was wishing us fair winds and a successful voyage.

Ralph Salmon, our interpreter, made a little speech expressing our gratitude. The headman in turn replied with dignified formality:

"We are sorry you cannot stay to enjoy our company. We have liked you. Now that you must leave us, we salute you and wish you good fortune on your long journey. May friendly winds take you quickly to your own people, and away from your enemy. When the war is over and you have defeated them, come back to see us and we shall have another feast."

Blessings and good wishes were lavished on us all the way to the prahu. The former crew insisted on coming aboard and setting the sails for us. Then they cast off and began poling us across the bar.

The four Malay sailors were a picturesque sight as they worked silhouetted against the last light of day. Full ahead the sun in all its fiery glory was descending into the sea.

The skipper and I were lounging against the deckhouse, relishing the fresh evening breeze.

"This would be a bit of all right—if we didn't have the Japs breathing down our necks," the skipper said.

I nodded.

"Wouldn't it, though?"

He glanced down at the Malays.

"I'll bet you never started on an ocean race like this before."

"I'll tell you this," I replied. "I never set out on one where the stakes were so high."

Hooper's tanned face was serious.

"Yes—freedom and our lives—those are high stakes, all right."

A little way down the deck Limey was leaning his elbows on the rail. Suddenly he began to recite:

> *"Sunset and evening star*
> *And one clear call for me*
> *May there be no moaning at the bar*
> *When I set out to sea."*

"He's thinking of all those unpaid chits at Raffles bar in Singapore," said Anzac with a grin.

"I imagine he left a few of those behind," the skipper chuckled.

There was a burst of laughter. The tension, which had been building up with our departure, eased.

We were over the bar now. The Malays lifted their poles, lashed them to the side of the deckhouse, and climbed over the rail into their dugout canoe which the prahu had been towing behind.

They cast off and stood up, bidding us farewell in an elaborate pantomime which combined good wishes with sharp sallies.

"Whoever heard of soldiers sailing their own boat?" their gestures seemed to say. "Now you have only wind and water to fight. But since you must fight them—fight well!"

Quickly it became night. A gentle zephyr eased us out to sea. We were on our way.

The skipper was at the tiller. He puffed silently on his pipe and gazed contentedly over the Indian Ocean.

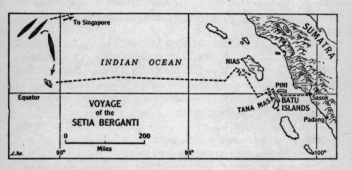

After a time he called us together to set the shipboard routine. To Anzac, also a master mariner, he gave responsibility for the navigation. I was to be second mate. Each watch was made up of three. The colonel and Ralph Salmon were assigned to my watch. Hooper was to have the first watch, I, the middle watch, and Anzac, the morning watch. Since Limey was not yet fit for heavier work, he was made paymaster and cook.

The skipper looked me over, taking stock of my large frame and ruddy Scottish complexion.

"You're a healthy-looking type," he said. "I'm going to call you Rosie."

In the chaotic conditions that ensued after the fall of Singapore, men from all the services, from all the nations of the Commonwealth, met briefly, were thrown together for a time, and then parted. We seldom knew a man's full name. We gave each other generic nicknames and the nicknames stuck. A man from London was given the tag of "Limey"; an Australian was known as "Aussie"; and so on. Thus I became known as "Rosie."

Soon a singing wind came from the east. With "a bone in our teeth" we sped on our course. When I was called at midnight to stand my watch, I found we were making a good seven knots.

No moon shone, but the silver brilliance of the stars lighted the white foam of the waves to make it glow. The quietness around us was so different from the abrupt silence which comes sometimes in the midst of battle. It was the quietness of a pleasing symphony—a symphony of wind, and water gurgling in friendly fashion along the hull.

Up there on the afterdeck underneath the stars, with the sense of speed coming through the tremor of the tiller, I had the feeling that it was great to be alive.

"This is the life!" I said impulsively to the colonel who was on deck with me.

"It's all right, isn't it?" he replied quietly. "Like standing apart from the world—as though you're in another dimension. I suppose it's the movement of the boat and the vastness of the sea that does it."

"I know one thing," I said. "It makes it easy to forget all the fighting in Malaya, the fires, the smoke and blood of Singapore—the escape route to Sumatra. They all seem a long way off now, don't they?"

"Now they do," he said thoughtfully. "But we can't leave those memories behind forever. We may suppress them for a while. But I expect we'll always have them."

All went well through the next day. The following dawn our kindly wind left us, and we were at the mercy of an awkward sea. Sharp puffs came up from every quarter, only to die down again.

It was my watch below, but I could not sleep. In the hold, every sound from abovedeck was greatly amplified—the flap of the sails, the crack of booms, the rattle of the blocks.

Suddenly there was a steep, heavy lurch. With it came the heartbreaking sound of canvas ripping. On deck all was chaos.

The dreaded accidental jibe had taken place. In the course of it, the mainsail had been caught by the mizzen, and it was rent from head to foot, clew to throat, leech to luff. In place of the bellying sail that had been hurrying us along, a pitiful bundle of shreds hung lifeless from the mainmast.

Not a word was spoken. No one gave voice to the fear that was in his heart: "Does this mean that we're not going to make it after all?" We put on a good face, smiled encouragingly to one another, and gathered in the bits and pieces. All was not lost. The jib, staysail, and mizzen were still intact. To these we added a spare jib which we set on the mainmast.

I stared dismally at the remnants lying on the deck. I said to the skipper,

"It's no better than a bunch of diapers. Do you think we'll ever be able to make a mainsail from that?"

"We'll have to try," he said grimly.

And try we did. All that day we sewed, stitching rag to rag with the patience of desperation while we wallowed in a heavy sea. At last we hoisted the makeshift sail. It held. We permitted ourselves a faint cheer.

We were on the move again. Later that night the wind steadied and freshened enough to take us along at about four knots.

The time came for my watch. I was on deck, looking out to sea, when I thought I saw something. I called the skipper.

"Look!" I said. "Off the starboard bow. There are two small islands where they shouldn't be."

The skipper looked, and said with a yawn,

"We're probably skirting the outer fringe of the Batus. Bound to be a few coral islands about. I can't think it's anything to worry us. Keep your eyes skinned. I'm going below to finish my sleep."

I was not at all happy. Islands were likely to be ringed with coral reefs whose sharp teeth could chew into our hull.

We had no charts of these waters. Our navigational aids, on a par with those of sailing-ship days, consisted of a compass, a school atlas in Dutch (which none of us could read), and a naval book of nautical tables. We calculated our position daily by means of our day's work. That is, we averaged our course, distance, and leeway and worked out our position with the aid of the log tables. We could no more than approximate where we were at any given time.

The islands passed by to starboard. I could hear the soughing of the waves embracing them.

My watch came to an end. Still worried about our position, I turned in. My sleep, however, was soon rudely broken by the thump of running feet. But what alarmed me was the sound of booming surf, smashing against a lee shore. I rushed on deck and saw much too near us a mass of frothing foam.

Then I heard two splashes. The men on watch had let go both anchors and were paying out the hawsers. I joined in. We made them fast to the bits and waited. The anchors held. We were safe for the time being.

Within an hour dawn came. Our pulses slowed at what we saw. On all sides of us waves were breaking into white bubbles over atolls and coral reefs. But we were afloat and within calm waters. Miraculously, we had sailed into a lagoon. The day was strengthening; the view was beautiful: a succession of green, palm-fringed islands bordered with white beaches rose from the emerald-and-sapphire sea. We carried an eleven-foot dugout canoe lashed to the foredeck. We lowered it over the side. The colonel, Salmon the interpreter, and I got in. We paddled along the lagoon until we came to an inlet where we could see a cluster of palm-leaf huts. We beached the canoe. A large family of what appeared to be fisherfolk came out to greet us.

We learned through Salmon that we were on an island named Pini. This was only a small settlement, however; the head village was four or five miles away. The skipper decided that I should take Salmon and go seek the headman's help in getting us out of the lagoon. Two of the fishermen volunteered to paddle us over.

One of them, a kind of patriarch, had only one eye. We nicknamed him Nelson. He used his empty socket with devastating effect, turning it full upon us whenever he questioned our intelligence. This was often. Age, sun, and sea had made his face a thing of wrinkled splendor. A permanent leering grin rounded off his character, giving him a lusty, villainous mien. While we paddled, with Salmon's help I struck up a conversation with him.

"Have you lived here most of your life?"

"All of my life, naturally."

"What do you do?"

"I fish. What else would I do?"

"Do you like working at sea?"

"Oh, yes. I know all about the sea. I understand it. I take fish from it. We get on well together."

He bobbed his head and screwed up his one good eye wisely as he said this.

"Silly," he seemed to be implying. "Can't you see I know my trade? See how I paddle this canoe! See how I can tell the ways of the water! The ocean and I are one!"

After crossing a brilliant blue bay, we could see the village.

The headman was already moving gracefully down the beach toward us. His white baju and sarong blended with the glistening white sand in the sunlight, so that he seemed only face and arms and legs and feet. We shook hands in easy friendship.

"Come to my hut," he said, "and I will refresh you."

The hut was spacious and clean. The few furnishings were neatly in order.

The headman's wife brought us clear coffee in glasses and a basket of small sweet bananas.

We were describing our predicament when his wife returned, bearing a delicious meal of fried chicken, fried fish, steaming rice, and a tray of empty bowls.

This was an enchanting interlude. Our host and hostess treated us with friendly courtesy, anticipating our every want. We made no attempt to hurry our conversation. We told them about the war, how we were escaping from the Japanese, how we had ripped our mainsail, repaired it as best we could, and how we had miraculously found our way through the reefs into the quiet waters of the lagoon.

"Our great need at the moment is for sails, rope, and a pilot," I told the headman.

"I cannot give you rope or sails," he said, "but I shall be delighted to pilot you to Tana Masa, another larger island lying forty miles to the west. There you will be able to buy rope and other gear."

When we returned to our base at the edge of the lagoon we were greeted with a scene of frenzied activity. Eight fishermen were seated with our crewmates in a circle on the sand, arms going furiously. They had pegged out on the ground the bolts of cotton I had bought in Sasok and were stitching them together into a sail. We sat down and joined in.

Darkness fell. Someone fetched a lantern from the prahu and we worked on by its light, with stiff fingers, aching muscles, and strained eyes. It was almost midnight when we finished.

We passed our cigarettes among the fishermen. "Tailor-mades" did not often come their way and they were voluble in their gratitude.

We all lay down to rest on the beach. It seemed I had only dozed off when I felt a tap on my shoulder. I roused myself to see Nelson's baleful socket fixed on me. He had come before dawn to volunteer to go with us to Tana Masa as our sailing master.

Speedily we bent on the new mainsail and stowed the repaired one as a spare. The first light of the new day was just edging the sky when off to starboard we saw the headman's outrigger ghosting toward us in an air so light we could hardly feel it. In a moment he hailed us.

"I've come to pilot you to Tana Masa. Follow me when you are ready. Perhaps there will be wind when the sun rises."

We set sail and weighed anchor, but we did not move. No puff of wind could we find anywhere. Finally came a breath that nudged the prahu—enough so we could follow the headman's outrigger.

I stood with Limey at the taffrail, enjoying the beauty around us. We looked down into the water. It was crystal clear and sparkling blue—a bluer blue than I had seen anywhere. Turrets and minarets of every color formed fascinating coral cities. Through them schools of well-fed fish patrolled at leisure.

The clamor of war seemed far away. Island after island passed our beam as we drifted gently along. Coconut palms fringing the coral shores suggested cool breezes and a life of gracious ease. It was all very tempting. The waters abounded with fish and the islands with tasty fruits of a wide variety. Why struggle to push on? Why not bribe the natives with our remaining cigarettes to build us one of their palm-leaf huts and live on here among these kind and generous people until the war was over?

I told Limey of my thoughts.

"How about it?" he said, winking at me. "If we do reach Ceylon, you know very well we'll be pushed into some bloody mess or other the minute we get there. Why not stay and be lords of these isles? We'll fish and hunt like gentlemen, and in our spare time we'll brew coconut brandy. Then we'll settle back in our hammocks in our palm-leaf palaces and wait for lovely dusky princesses to come courting us!"

The colonel farther down the rail was listening.

"Wouldn't that be glorious!" he exclaimed. "And we'd go on from island to island. Think—we could win an empire by living, while everyone else is losing theirs—by dying!"

The skipper joined in:

"By gum, we could train monkeys to be our servants! Intelligent little buggers, they are, you know."

Limey picked up this train of thought.

"We could rig up a big fan. Have them pull it with their tails, as they swing to and fro. While we lie there on our soft beds with our mouths open, waiting for the ripe fruit to drop in, they'd be working like nailers to keep us cool."

Suddenly the skipper straightened up and peered toward the horizon.

"What's that?"

We could make out a dark speck. It might be enemy. On the other hand, it might be a friendly ship.

"It's too far off—they'll never see us," said Limey.

"Oh, I don't know about that," said Anzac. "Here, I've a mirror. Try signaling with it, Skipper."

Hooper knelt on the deck, took the mirror in his hand and proceeded to flash signals. We waited. The sun flashed back signals of its own on the sparkling water. Our eyes, however, were well enough trained by now to distinguish between the fancied and the real; no signal was coming from the ship.

The smudge had gone. Long after there was nothing to see, the skipper kept on signaling. At last he gave up. He leaned down and rested the mirror against the rail. When he straightened up to stretch himself, he kicked the mirror with his foot. It fell forward. He knelt to pick it up. It was broken in two.

"See what you've done!" moaned Limey. "You've broken the bloody thing. Seven years' bad luck for all of us—that's what it is!"

We stared at the broken mirror. We knew we were not superstitious. Luck was what you did with what you had. It was what you made for yourself—by yourself—for good or ill. And yet . . .

Anzac was a steady type. "It isn't as though it had been smashed to smithereens, you know. It's only broken in two," he said in his cool, slow voice. "That's only three and a half years' bad luck. Maybe those are the ones behind us. You wouldn't exactly call Singapore lucky, would you?"

He picked up the two halves and took them below.

While we were waiting for the wind to freshen we fished. We had only bent pins for hooks and balls of rice for bait. In the clear sunlit water we could see our rice balls dangling before the fishes' noses. They looked at the bait, then continued haughtily on their way.

We heard Nelson laughing behind us.

"It's no use," he said, tapping Salmon on the shoulder. "They'll never catch any fish that way."

"Show us how, then," we pleaded. Nelson only shrugged. "All right, will you catch some for us yourself?"

Nelson remained adamant. He considered it beneath him to share his secrets with such rank amateurs.

For two days we lazed our way through the reefs, moving in the right direction, but slowly—so slowly.

On the third morning we decided to put Nelson to the test.

"Look here—if you're so cozy with the elements, why don't you prove it and bring us a wind?"

"Oh, I shall," said Nelson, fixing his empty socket on us.

His method could hardly have been simpler. All that he did was to step to the rail, turn his blind eye in the direction from which he wished the wind to come, draw in a great chestful of air, and then roar, "Hroosh! Hroosh!"

Aeolus, the wind god, or his southeastern representative, must have heard Nelson and honored the request. Very shortly there were ripples on the water. Before long the sails were filling under a full-bodied breeze. We made Tana Masa by noon, averaging eight knots on the run. Our respect for Nelson and his lore rose considerably.

We sailed straight to the jetty and tied up. At the sight of the prahu a crowd of natives ran down the beach to greet us. But when they saw we were white men instead of the expected Malays they turned and fled. Presently, from a distance, they concluded that our mission, strange though it might be, was a peaceful one and they began straggling back toward us. By this time the headman had arrived from Pini and was haranguing them. After a while he broke away and came up to the ship.

"They'll be glad to help you," he said with a friendly grin. "You have but to tell them what you need."

We did, and soon had a supply of rope and sailcloth.

Then Sandy, the other interpreter from the Malay Volunteer Force who had a pretty good understanding of the island dialects, reported that he had found a carpenter in possession of some planking who was willing to build us a sleeping deck in the hold.

The next morning, while we were busy rerigging the ship, we saw a Malay wearing the white ducks of authority running toward us. When he could get his breath he explained that he was the controller and wanted us to help him put down a war between two tribes. After our long series of defeats elsewhere we were flattered by his request.

The colonel asked if the natives were armed with rifles. The controller told us that the Netherlands Government did not permit natives to have firearms. They were, however, armed with parangs, thin knifelike swords about three feet long.

We held a conference.

"We've got to support the poor chap," the colonel said. "Otherwise, he won't have any authority after we leave. Law and order here depend upon his ability to command assistance whenever he needs it."

"That's right," agreed Limey. "Just you chaps push off and settle it. Someone's got to stay behind and mind the ship. That's me."

It didn't take us long to prepare. We donned our khaki drill and buckled on our revolvers.

"Now isn't this something!" observed Crawley, the young curly-haired gunner, as we mustered on the jetty. "Among the handful of us here, we represent six branches of the services— Navy, Artillery, Infantry, Engineers, Signals, and Service Corps—all we're lacking is the Air Force."

"Find me the Air Force and I'll take off in one of their planes," Limey called from the prahu.

The controller led the way to the battlefield.

We passed a long, low hut filled with rows of pallets. Moans and cries of pain were coming from it.

"Who's in there?" one of us asked.

"Oh, those are the wounded," the controller answered with what seemed to us rather too much pride. Crawley went over, put his head in, and came back to report.

"Crickey, the place is full," he said. "Some have bloody

bandages on their heads. Some of 'em are cut up pretty badly. I saw one of their parangs. Nasty-looking weapon it is, too."

We continued on our way.

"Hey," Crawley asked the controller, "how many fighting men are there on each side?"

"Oh, about three hundred, I should say."

"Crumbs!" exclaimed Crawley. "What if they don't like the idea of our interfering in their war and join sides against us? Six hundred to nine is heavy odds."

We reached the front. It was only a clearing where one row of Malays with drawn parangs stood glaring unhappily at another row, also with drawn parangs. Briskly and confidently we marched down between the two rows of warriors, staring them insolently in the eye while keeping our hands on our revolvers.

We could think of nothing to do but to stand there looking fierce and warlike. By twos and threes the Malays began to slip out of line and melt away into the jungle. We held our position until the last warrior had vanished.

The colonel then suggested to the controller that if he could obtain the consent of the warring chiefs, we would undertake to mediate their dispute.

The controller was delighted and led us at once to the compound of one of the warring factions, composed of a hollow square of huts. Opposite the main gate was a large council chamber of impressive splendor. Built on heavy piles, it towered to a height of about one hundred and fifty feet at the peak of its atap palm roof which narrowed to an elegant point made of finely carved wood. In front of the hall were several stone chairs, set up as though for a council meeting, and two stone altars. A large footprint was carved on top of one of the altars, suggesting an ancient Hindu origin.

The council hall itself was arranged like the interior of a medieval castle, with the common room at one end and a raised platform at the other. The chief welcomed us. He was a rather grand-looking, tall old man whose ears had been pierced and the holes enlarged to hold a small coin. When we were all seated in a semicircle he clapped his hands and ordered that green coconuts be brought for our refreshment. We in turn handed around our cigarettes. The palaver was ready to begin.

"Oh, yes, I am of the opinion that war is a very bad thing. I do not want war. My tribe does not want war. But," he added, unconsciously echoing the shibboleth common to all mankind, "how can we live at peace with our neighbors when our neighbors want war and are always making war?" He shook his head; the decorations flashed in his ear lobes. A look of perplexity wrinkled his wise face.

"It is all very difficult," he sighed. "It is all very difficult."

The colonel conceded that indeed it was—then promptly presented our offer to mediate with the rival tribe. The chief readily accepted. We set out for the other compound, taking him with us, followed by his chattering entourage.

We found this compound was a striking contrast to the first. The council hall was a ruin, the huts dilapidated. There was refuse in the streets, and a general air of slackness prevailed.

We also noted a marked difference between the two chiefs. Whereas the first was vigorous, authoritative, and dignified, this one was ancient, slovenly, and wily.

The peace conference ritual began, and once again coconuts and cigarettes were exchanged. The colonel, having had the benefit of a rehearsal, was at the top of his form. His eloquent argument sounded irrefutable to us. But evidently not so to the rival chief.

That worthy listened impassively until the colonel had finished, and then stated his case.

"But of course," he began, "nonaggression has been my unfailing policy. I am a man of the highest principles and I have always stood by them. We have been forced to defend ourselves against the aggressive acts of the other tribe. They are so wicked there is nothing left for us but to show them the error of their ways by our superior strength."

He looked at the colonel shrewdly.

"Why is it that you white men take such an interest in our war? You have a war of your own which has been going on for some time, do you not?"

The colonel admitted that this was true.

"How did your war begin?" the colonel inquired.

"A young man from the other tribe insulted one of our young women," the chief replied.

"And when did this incident take place?"

"About forty years ago."

The recollection of that indignity rekindled a slumbering rage in the chief. His eyes flashed anew with anger. The colonel reasoned with him and eventually he calmed down enough to agree to keep the peace—for the time being, at any rate. But not even an offer of twenty cigarettes could persuade him to shake hands with his enemy. We had, however, saved face for the controller. Mission accomplished, we returned to our prahu and made ready for our departure.

We were weighing anchor, when we spotted two natives paddling toward us at top speed. Speaking rapidly and gesticulating excitedly, they told us they had sighted a Japanese gunboat steaming up between the islands in our direction. They assured us we had no cause for worry. They would pilot us to a creek surrounded by trees where the enemy would never see us.

This was all very well, except that there was not a whiff of wind—only dead flat calm. Fortunately we had six long oars. We manned them and pulled like galley slaves. The *Setia Berganti* was an inert weight. The sun blazed down on the lagoon. Sweat poured from us in gallons; our lungs ached. But the prahu began to move. Fathom by fathom, cable by cable, we moved her over the three miles until we were hidden behind the palm trees. From our safe haven we peered out and watched the Japanese vessel pass us, unaware of our presence. We were happy to see she was on a course opposite to our own.

Two hours later the "all clear" was given. Once more we manned the oars. But a breeze had risen, the sails filled, and we pointed the bow toward open waters.

When we came abeam of our former berth, the headman from Pini joined us in his outrigger. He sailed with us for about an hour. Then he came alongside to shake our hands and wish us a safe voyage. With a final wave and the farewell cry of "salamat jalan" he set his course for the east, while we sailed westward. We felt a deep sense of loss as we watched his outrigger point toward the distant islands. Although we had few things in common, he had been a true friend.

Our island interlude was over. As we watched the last sight of land disappear, we spoke no more of our dreams of a life of ease in that tropical paradise. We were all anxious again to get on with it—to make our way to Ceylon and freedom. Our mainsail was sound; we had a spare one; there was plenty of coconut, and fresh fruit in the hold. We had something resembling proper bunk space. In fact, both we and the *Setia Berganti* were in better shape than we had been for a long while.

Rather thankfully, we resumed the regularity of shipboard routine, passing the days standing our watches, mending sail, and tidying ship.

From time to time we indulged in good-humored complaints about our meals. Limey was not the least bit put out. His standard reply was, "Well, you know what you can do, don't you?" It was difficult to find a winning answer to his question. But our mess was not bad. We started the day with a hot breakfast of boiled rice; followed it with a cold luncheon of left-over rice with fruit or coconut; ended it with a hot dinner of rice and tinned beef.

When we had been in action biscuits and canned beef were our regular ration and one I thought I'd never want to see again. But now it tasted superb, perhaps because the sea air gave me such a good appetite. The only sad part was that the beef was in short supply. It would not last many more days.

To our dismay, we found that our water, too, was getting low. The burning heat, the unremitting glare of the sun on the sea, and the salt air gave us a parching thirst. Often in my dreams I could imagine myself kneeling down on the moors at home to drink from some ice-cold highland spring. The water on the ship was unpleasantly flavored by the oil or gasoline from the tins and barrels in which it had been stored. Until now, I had not known that good fresh water has a taste —a taste of sweetness.

Our water was diminishing faster than we were drinking it. We could see that we were sustaining losses at a dangerous rate through evaporation and leakage. We rationed ourselves to a pint apiece every twenty-four hours, hoping thereby to make the water last until either we reached our destination or were picked up.

But once we got through the day we had the better side of life. Each evening after sundown we gathered on deck for a pleasant social hour. I can see it yet—the sun gilding the sky with its afterglow, the slow, soothing, gentle swelling of the sea as we sat together and joked and smoked and talked.

Often these conversations centered on our postwar plans. One evening the sun had just made its dignified bow over the horizon, leaving us to the half light and half shadow that mark the interval between day and night on shipboard. The

Setia Berganti sailed along effortlessly on the ever-rising, ever-falling bosom of the ocean.

This was a time of leisure and of peace. The wind was with us and was gently pushing us on our way. Anzac lolled beside the tiller. Limey, having finished with his galley chores, joined us where we sat cross-legged on the afterdeck or lounged against the rooftop of the hold.

"A glorious great foaming gallon of iced beer's all I need now," said Limey as he squatted down beside me.

"That—and the absence of Japs," put in Anzac.

"Otherwise we've just about everything," Limey said. Then, anticipating a protest, he added quickly, "Oh, I know what you're thinking—no women. For the younger chaps, that is —for Crawley here—and Rosie."

That was his joke—for Limey talked more than any of us of the women who would be waiting for him in Colombo. We all grinned. His banter expressed what we were feeling: Life at this moment was good.

The colonel was sitting with his elbows on his knees and his chin in his hands. His pipe, dangling from his mouth, swung gently to and fro in motion with the prahu.

"It's all rather pleasant, I must admit," he said with characteristic geniality. "Made so by pleasant sailing companions. Might be fun to repeat this cruise after the war. How about you, Limey? What'll you be doing then?"

Limey replied without hesitation. He had made his plans.

"Oh, I'll be in the City during the day, making me packet. Then at night you'll doubtless find me in the local knocking it back with the old soaks. After that I'll make it home to the wife and kids—all in due time—if I have any by then."

With a shake of the head he concluded,

"No, I won't be doing any cruising. Not in these waters anyway."

"Skipper, how about you?"

"Afraid you can count me out. I've responsibilities. It's back to Singapore for me as fast as I can make it, once I've stopped by to pick up my family in South Africa. That's where I sent them when I was mobilized."

"And you, Rosie?"

"You can count me in," I said. "I'll probably be wandering around anyway."

"Don't you have any definite plans?" the skipper inquired with surprise.

"Nearest I have to a plan is the Army," I said. "Just before the Japs started their nonsense I was nominated for an appointment to Staff College at Quetta, in India. Maybe I'll be able to start with the next course. If I do I'll stay on in the service."

"You could do worse," said the colonel. "I've found it very satisfying."

"Isn't there something else you'd like to do?" the skipper asked.

I thought a minute.

"There is one other thing. After the occupation, there's going to be a bit of a mess around here. The Japs will have to get out of Java and Sumatra. We'll give Malaya and India more independence. This'll mean that local nabobs will be looking for military and political advisers. I might take care to be around when the booking begins."

"What? Not planning to become another Raffles, are you?" Anzac raised his eyebrows. (Raffles was a British gentleman adventurer, famous in the East, who founded Singapore.)

"If I should happen to follow in the footsteps of chaps like Raffles, why should I mind?" I said. "Especially if I could make a fortune doing it. I am thinking of working behind the scenes, sort of, in the field of power politics. The best place in that game is the back room: that's where the controls are."

"Sounds to me as though you've got it all worked out," remarked Anzac mildly, looking up from his compass.

"Not the details. That'll come later. A man has to give a little thought, though, as to where he's most likely to get the butter for his bread, the caviar to go with his champagne."

"Now you're talking sense," Limey chimed in. "Maybe I'll change my mind and join your cruise after all—*if* you'll provide a great ruddy steam yacht with caviar by the bucket and gallons of champagne. That's *my* idea of cruising."

"Not mine," said Anzac. "I'll be content with a fair day's wage for a fair day's work, three meals a day, and a roof over my head."

"You're crazy!" snorted Limey. "I'm all in favor of Rosie's idea. When he gets his job as Adviser-in-Chief to the Sultan of Somewhere, I'm going to join him as Chief Adviser to the Adviser-in-Chief. Between us we'll rake in the dough and live a gloriously sinful life of ease and luxury for the rest of our days."

Anzac wagged his big head slowly in disapproval and observed quietly,

"The pair of you sound to me like a couple of ruthless rascals."

I had great respect for Anzac as a seaman, but I thought his views on life dull and stuffy.

"Not ruthless," I retorted. "Realistic. It's the chaps who *know* that we live in a tough world and that you've got to be tough to survive who do the leading." I turned to Limey to support my position. "Right, Limey?"

"That's right—too right—too bloody right."

Anzac was unruffled by our loud-voiced protestations. He replied in his same calm, detached tone,

"Money—and power—and success—they aren't everything, y'know."

"Oh, aren't they?" I jeered.

"No, they aren't. There's such a thing as decency."

Limey shrugged. "Trouble with you, Anzac, is that you're too bloody good for—too bloody good for—too good for your own good."

He seemed satisfied that he had the last word. He got up, yawned, and went below, leaving Anzac to the tiller, the stars —and his thoughts.

Our spirits rose with each passing day. We talked with confidence of what we would do when we reached Ceylon. The Japanese and their threat to us were almost forgotten. Every sunrise was bringing us thirty or forty miles closer to our landfall and to freedom.

We were enjoying our life at sea, when fever struck us. One by one we were confined to our bunks below. It was increasingly difficult to make up the complement of a watch. At first we did not know what malady might be loose among us. But finally it became clear that only those had it who had gone ashore to sew sail at Pini. Also, the cases began to display common malarial symptoms.

I came on deck every day, took my place at the tiller, and scorned the others' misfortunes. Then, on one afternoon watch, I felt peculiar myself. Everything began to rotate in front of me. I looked at the compass. It rushed backward and forward at me. I looked up. Sky and sea cavorted in a mad dance. Nothing was stable, everything was in flux. When I felt myself flying through space, I knew it was time to quit.

The colonel saw me slumped by the tiller. He called for help to carry me below deck. There he took my temperature, and whistled "Whew!"

It was hot, cramped, and dark in the hold. The smells of former cargoes, of dried fish and coconut, enfolded me in layers of hot, sticky air. But I was conscious of very little as I lay there on my bunk with a raging temperature.

When my fever abated, the first thing that impressed itself

on my consciousness was not the smells, not the fetid air, but the fact that we were moving—moving through the water at a steady, reasonable speed.

One evening I was able to make my appearance on deck at the social hour. After my long period of delirium and isolation this was an occasion. My shipmates welcomed me warmly. I thought I noticed a new optimism among them. They laughed easily and spoke more definitely of what we would do when we reached Ceylon. I wondered at this change. Presently the skipper said,

"Tell Rosie the good news, Anzac."

"By my reckoning, Rosie," said Anzac, "we are now clear of the danger area. I'd say we're within five hundred miles of our goal. With a bit of luck," he continued, beaming, "a Royal Naval Patrol may flag us at any minute—and we'll be quids in."

"Won't we, though!" Limey crowed. "Quids in and quids out! I'm going to spend all my back pay on a party. It's going to be a whopper. I may even ask you, Rosie."

The colonel stood up.

"Why wait to celebrate?" he asked. "Why not have the party now?"

"With what?" Limey wanted to know.

"It so happens that I have in my kit a bottle of quite old Tokay. It should be rather good. I'll break it out right now."

Murmurs of incredulity followed him as he went below. We wondered how he had come by that bottle in the first place and what had prompted him to take it along in his stripped-down gear, hoarding it for the appropriate moment to celebrate. Limey went to fetch some tin cups. The colonel returned with the bottle in his hand. Going around the circle, he poured us each a dram.

"Here's to Colombo!" He raised his cup in a toast.

"On to Colombo!" we all roared in one voice.

Limey glanced up at the curving sails, then out at our wake.

"Think of it! At the rate we're going we should hit Ceylon inside of a week!"

We dared think about it now. I visualized Colombo as I had last seen it, when I had gone through there in the early months of 1940 on my way to Malaya. I remembered the thronging docks, the low white buildings along the well-ordered streets, the waving palm trees, the red rickshaws, and the policemen in spic-and-span uniforms. I could see Colombo now, waiting to welcome us. The scene was so vivid I could almost reach out and touch it.

The wine tasted refreshingly sweet. The hour ended. We rose from our huddled positions on deck, shook the cramps from our legs, and went below to give ourselves over to our dreams. Only the helmsman remained at his post.

The following day I had come up to clear my lungs in the fresh morning air when I heard the watch cry out,

"Smoke ho!"

Over on the starboard side I could see a heavy smudge low on the horizon. By this time we were all on deck.

"That's three ships!" the skipper shouted.

"Right. I can see the funnels," I called.

"Shall we signal?" someone asked.

"No! No!" said the skipper. "They still might be enemy." He turned to the helmsman. "Go on opposite course," he said hurriedly. "Even if they are they may think we're only wandering Chinese or Malays."

The skipper had an inspiration.

"Sapper!"

"Yes, old boy?"

"Think you can steer for a while?"

"I think so."

"You're the shorty of the outfit. Get into that coolie coat

and that big straw hat and take the tiller. The rest of you go below."

The Sapper disappeared; within moments he came back, wearing his disguise. In his wide conical straw hat and long jacket he looked so authentically Oriental as he took his position by the tiller that we all laughed in spite of our uncomfortable situation.

By now we were gathered in the smelly hold. With beating hearts and constricted stomachs we waited. All we could see through the hatchway was the Sapper's coolie hat against the vast gray expanse of the morning sky.

"What are they, can you see yet?" the skipper called out.

"Not quite. They're three ships. That's all I can see."

No one stirred. Only the slap of water could be heard against the sides of the hold. Then came the Sapper's voice:

"They look like tankers . . . Yes, they are tankers. I'm sure they are."

"Are they enemy?" called the colonel.

"Can't tell yet."

"I'm afraid they must be," said the skipper. "What would our tankers be doing in these waters?"

This made sense. Our first hope—that they might be British or American warships—faded. Now we clung hard to another —the hope that the ships would pass us by. A hum of conversation arose as we tried to reassure ourselves. What if they were Japanese? Why should they concern themselves with an old prahu and a Malay crew?

"Where are they now?" the skipper asked.

"They're still coming in our direction."

The Sapper said nothing. We held our breath. Then,

"Still coming . . . still coming . . . still coming. . . they're about a mile off . . . they're abeam . . . they're enemy all right, blast it! . . . they're drawing away from us . . . still drawing away . . . still drawing away . . . they're well past us . . ."

"With a bit of luck we might make it yet," said Limey.

"We just might," we all murmured.

"Oh, my God!" the Sapper groaned. "One of them is turning!"

I peered over the rail and saw a tanker steaming toward us, her prow throwing up a wave of snarling white water. I could tell from the slack postures of my comrades that their hopes, like mine, had reached nadir. My stomach felt full of ice —cold, hard, raw.

We had failed.

I saw the flash of the four-inch gun on the foredeck. I heard the sharp crack of the explosion. Then there was a *whish* overhead. About fifty yards away a column of water spurted on our beam as the shell struck.

It was all up. Hastily, we threw our logbooks overside and our lead bullets after them. We readied our packs and wearily mustered on deck.

We waited in utter despair.

The tanker which had fired on us hove within hailing distance. The rails were lined with sailors—Japanese sailors.

"What a bloody awful sight!" said Limey. "Look at them, hanging over the sides staring at us."

"They're armed to the teeth," I said as my glance strayed upward. A whole battery of light guns and machine guns was trained upon us. "You'd think we were a battleship."

An officer in a white uniform bellowed at us through a megaphone to come alongside.

The skipper took the tiller. The rest of us trimmed sail for the last time. Smartly we sailed up to the tanker, luffed, and brought the prahu within reach of the rope ladder that had been lowered in the meantime.

The ship's side towered above us. A multitude of silent faces glared down on us.

"Make sure you take all your kit with you!" the skipper said. It was his last command.

One by one we clambered up the rope ladder. It was a long, hard climb, with packs and bundles bumping against our sides and becoming entangled with the swaying steps.

About halfway to the deck I looked below. My throat tightened. Sails set, alone and crewless, the *Setia Berganti* was edging away out over the ocean.

On deck two sailors grabbed me roughly. They twisted my arms behind my back. We were all searched; then we were passed into the safekeeping of personal guards. Mine was a nervous petty officer, who kept the muzzle of his automatic pistol pressed tightly against my head. It hurt. I was aware only of a blur of white uniform, a brown-yellow face, and a ring of steel against my skull.

"This isn't getting us anywhere," I thought to myself. So I said in my most persuasive voice,

"Look here, chum, relax, will you? If you'll take that thing away from my head, we'll both be more comfortable."

My well intended remark drew only a muttered: "Curra-abgeroshksshsgrhh!" The automatic was pressed all the more tightly. Standing, my head strained as far forward as humanly possible without losing my balance, I could see the skipper being escorted to the bridge. I noticed an officer coming my way.

"Please," I begged. "Tell my friend here I'm not going to escape and that I won't hurt him."

The officer understood English. He barked a quick order; the sailor withdrew the pistol.

"Thanks, sir," I said. Then, taking heart from his gesture, I asked the officer, "What are you going to do with us?"

He stopped in front of me, placed his hands on his hips, and grinned expansively.

"You will all be questioned one at a time," he said in clipped artificial English, "and then you will be shot. You are spies!"

"That's cheerful news," I murmured as I rubbed my aching skull.

The skipper returned, looking glum. He was taken to the opposite side of the deck under guard so that he could not say anything to us.

All morning long our interrogation continued. In the afternoon my turn came. I was escorted to a large cabin on one of the bridges.

I stood facing three officers seated behind a table. Spread out upon it were personal possessions—watches, wallets, cigarettes, toilet kits, a camera, and pencils. Suddenly my heart flipped. I was looking at my blue leather wallet—the one my father had given to me when I left Scotland. I remembered what was in it. Why hadn't I destroyed that chit? Had they read it? Did they already know that I was formally authorized to raise money and collect arms to encourage resistance among the Malays?

Keeping a poker face, I bowed as stiffly and formally as though I were being presented at Buckingham Palace.

The three officers ducked their heads without rising.

"Who are you?"

"Ernest Gordon."

"What is your rank?"

"Captain."

"What is your regiment?"

"The Ninety-third Highlanders."

I was allowed to give this much information under Army regulations. But no more. From now on I would have to play it by ear. I had difficulty keeping my eyes away from the wallet.

"Why were you on the boat?"

"Because I didn't want to stay in Sumatra."

"Where were you before Sumatra?"

"Singapore."

The officer in the center fixed me with his hard eyes. He snapped out,

"Were you spying for the British Navy?"

"No."

The three officers held a whispered conference. They seemed satisfied with my answers. One of them said,

"Pick out your possessions."

It was all too pat. Were they playing cat and mouse with me? Could it be that they had found the chit and were letting me spring my own trap?

Assuming a *sang-froid* I did not feel, I stepped forward and picked up a pencil and one or two other objects. I reached for my wallet. I felt their eyes on me. At any moment I expected to hear one of them bark "Now!"

The silence prevailed. I picked up the wallet. Opening it, I pulled out several snapshots of girl friends and flashed them before the officers with a man-of-the-world air. They nodded understandingly.

"God bless the girl friends," I muttered, and returned the wallet to my pocket. I picked out my camera from which the film had been removed.

"You may go," the senior officer said.

I bowed and thankfully withdrew.

When I was back at my place on deck, I pantomimed to my guard that I had an urgent appointment in the head or "benjo." He had relaxed a little now, and nodded his permission. I rushed for the head like a man caught short. As soon as I closed the door, I extracted the incriminating note from its hiding place in the outside pocket of my wallet and flushed it joyfully out of my life.

The interviews were over. Once more the skipper was escorted to the bridge, while the rest of us stood about in uneasy silence. After what seemed a lifetime he returned. But now he looked pleased.

Our personal guards withdrew. Only one was left, standing some distance away. We could talk freely.

"It's all right, chaps," the skipper said. "The Nips have changed their minds. We're not to be shot after all. We are to be treated as prisoners of war and taken back to Singapore for further questioning. These orders will stand. They've come from Tokyo."

Our treatment improved considerably. We were permitted to move about the deck. Our captors allowed us to drink as much fresh water as we pleased. After so many weeks of our unpalatable stores, this was wonderful.

We drank our fill and lounged against the rail, gazing out at the ocean. I recalled my last glimpse of the *Setia Berganti* as I had watched her sail forlornly away from us.

I wondered about her fate. Would she sail on, alone and crewless, to wash up on the beach at Ceylon? Would she become another *Marie Celeste*, a mystery of the sea? Or a legendary ship like the *Flying Dutchman*? Would the green coconuts finally sprout so that she became a floating island somewhere in the Indian Ocean?

She had given us three extra months of freedom. In spite of tense moments our memories were mainly happy ones.

Would we fare as well?

Four days later we dropped anchor off Singapore. The contrast was awesome. When we had last seen it about three months before, Singapore was a city of the damned, with great flames from the burning oil tanks billowing skyward in an angry red along the shoreline. Now all was hushed and quiet. It was a city of the dead.

Before reaching Singapore, one of the English-speaking officers had told us that we would be subjected to further interrogation by the Kempei Tai, or military police.

The prospect did not exactly raise our spirits. But it was just as well for our peace of mind that we did not know what we learned later—namely, that the Kempei Tai delighted in the most depraved tortures. This was to be affirmed by the Allied prosecution at the war crimes trial of 1946 as follows:

"The whole of this case can be epitomized by two words— 'unspeakable horror.' "

The anticipated interrogation never took place. In fact, we were treated in the most casual way possible, since liaison between the Japanese Navy and Army was practically nonexistent, owing to interservice rivalry. After being ferried ashore we were dumped on a pier and left there. No one was on hand to meet us or to guard us.

We must have presented a sorry spectacle as we waited, wondering what the next move would be. We were bearded and barefoot and wore the most bizarre assortment of uniforms.

Two British naval P.O.W.'s were working on a dock nearby. One of them looked up from his toil and saw us. He called out,

"Cheer up, chums! It could have been worse!"

After a while a truck rumbled up and carted us off to the prison camp at Changi twelve miles away.

CHAPTER 3

Our Hosts

SO BEGAN MY THREE AND ONE-HALF YEARS AS A guest of the Japanese. Changi was but the first of a succession of camps in which we were confined. Although bleak enough, that camp was a paradise compared to those we were to know later.

During the four years they were in control, the Japanese military violated every civilized code. They murdered prisoners overtly by bayoneting, shooting, drowning, or decapitation; they murdered them covertly by working them beyond human endurance, starving them, torturing them, and denying them medical care.

They also had special refinements for those prisoners who did not comply with certain orders. Some were tortured by having their heads crushed in vises; some were filled up with water and then jumped on; some were tied to a tree by their thumbs; some were buried alive in the ground, or similarly treated in a variety of ways. The statistics tell their own story: four per cent of prisoners held by the Germans and Italians died, as compared to twenty-seven per cent of those in the hands of the Japanese. (The percentage in the prison camps along the River Kwai was much higher than this.)

It is difficult to keep these atrocities in perspective. They were the result of behavior codes fostered by the military for their own ends, codes such as Hakko Ichiu, Kodo, and Bushido.

These codes held that the Emperor was divine, that Japan was a divine country, that both had a divine mission to the world. Therefore, it was victory or death, and any cruelty could be condoned.

This vicious doctrine was unquestioningly accepted. Once the situation changed, an organized attempt was made to expunge these acts from the record, as indicated by two orders sent to all prison camp commandants on August 20, 1945. The first ruled that all documentary evidence of atrocities must be destroyed; the second commanded all personnel known to have been responsible for them to flee at the earliest possible moment and to vanish, leaving no trace.

Many of the tormentors among the Japanese military delighted in carrying out the mandate of their barbarous codes. But, in turn, the Japanese can point to the thousands of non-combatants killed or horribly burned by the dropping of the bombs on Hiroshima and Nagasaki.

Both sides undoubtedly justified their cruelties as serving to shorten the war. Millions in the Western world still see no connection between their own consciences and mass slaughter and accept no responsibility for those acts.

Changi was located at the east side of Singapore Island on the site of former British barracks. The buildings still stood, but they could accommodate no more than a thousand men. The camp was surrounded by a barbed-wire fence twelve feet high. Within the fence lived forty thousand prisoners, cut off from each other in separate compounds.

By the time we arrived, it was already a going concern. It had been in business for about three months. The Japanese had left to their captives the responsibility of administration. Officers were not permitted to show any insignia of rank, but they were allowed to command their own units. In this way the normal hierarchy of military life still held and prevented Changi from degenerating into a shambles of anarchy.

The resourceful prisoners had already done much to make their situation bearable. They had built shacks from discarded lumber and fitted them with bunks. They had made eating and drinking utensils from soup cans, and kettles for cooking out of oil drums. They made bedding of sorts from rice sacks. We required little clothing, for the temperatures were consistently warm.

I was pleased to find survivors of my battalion camped in one corner of the prison area. An old friend, Jack Hyslop, invited me to share his shack.

The Argylls were better off than most, benefiting from the talents of a gifted rations sergeant, Percy Evans, an old hand at conjuring necessities out of thin air. As I had arrived in Changi barefoot, he promptly came to my aid with a pair of socks and boots.

I adapted quickly to the life.

Morale in the camp was low for a number of reasons. The pain of defeat was keenly felt. Many believed that capture had been too readily accepted. The story going around at the time of surrender had it that the British general had given his word to Lt. Gen. Yamashita that the garrison would be handed over intact. I heard from several sources that it had been considered bad form to attempt an escape. Later on, the Japanese insisted that everyone sign a no-escape pledge. When the prisoners did not comply with this order immediately, they were marched into one corner of Changi and kept on a starvation diet until the order was obeyed.

Furthermore, the bulk of troops had just arrived in Singapore in time to be captured and were so overwhelmed by atrocity stories that they lived in fear and trembling. Such stories were not without foundation. Many of our troops left behind in the jungle had been bayoneted or shot upon capture. On Black Friday the Japanese had gone through Alexandra Hospital in Singapore, killing by bayonet all patients, doctors, and nurses. They had tied thousands of Chinese hand to hand and massacred them on the beaches or taken them out in barges to be drowned. There was nothing unpremeditated about such massacres; they were carried out according to a well-established pattern. By these actions the Japanese made it clear that they had no intention of abiding by either The Hague or the Geneva Conventions governing treatment of P.O.W.'s.

Another factor which contributed to low morale was the insufficiency of our diet. The basic ration was rice amounting to less than twelve ounces per man per day. Meat, flour, sugar, and salt were negligible. The rice was polished and therefore contained none of the vitamins, proteins, or minerals necessary to maintain health.

The immediate results of this starvation diet were hunger, general depression, and "blackouts." Next came the host of diseases caused by vitamin deficiency, such as beriberi and pellagra.

Still another factor was the prevalence of "bore-hole" rumors, so named because it was at the latrines that men heard them.

The rumors were excessively optimistic. For example, although ten of us had just come from the Indian Ocean where the Japanese Navy and Air Force were in complete control, we were told again and again with absolute conviction that the Americans and British had already recaptured Java and Sumatra, that a counterattack on Malaya was to be launched within a few days, and that we would soon be released.

A fresh crop of such rumors started up daily; no one ever knew exactly where they originated.

Perhaps a rumor would be invented by someone who wanted

to cheer up a chum. It would then be passed on and magnified by someone else for the same purpose. Before long it gained currency and spread throughout the camp, to return at last to the originator completely unrecognizable.

The net effect, however, of hopes raised only to be dashed, was disastrous.

Physically, life was not hard at this period. We either did chores around the camp—mostly of a housekeeping nature— or we were taken off in work parties to the city to clean up the debris of war or to sweat on the docks, loading loot onto Japanese ships.

Competition was keen for these jobs because they made it possible for prisoners to slip into the shops and buy food.

I had not been at Changi very long when I was assigned to lead such a party, loading captured ordnance bound for Tokyo. An officer from another unit whom I knew only slightly came to ask a favor of me. A friend of his was dying of beriberi. He thought that if I could bring him a jar of Marmite, a popular yeast compound rich in vitamin B, it might save the man's life. I wrote "Marmite" at the top of my shopping list.

It was my first time on such a work party, but the men knew the ropes well. While half of them pretended to load the ship, the other half systematically plundered the dockside warehouses. They had no difficulty diverting the Japanese guards with horseplay, incidents staged for that purpose, or bold-faced bribery.

We were well along in loading ship when one of the men in the looting detail touched my elbow.

"There's a case of Marmite back in the warehouse," he whispered. "But if you want some you'd better hurry."

I followed him down the dock and through the echoing interior of the warehouse between canyons of packing boxes. We came upon a group of P.O.W.'s who had just breached a case and were busy grabbing the contents. I pushed in among them in time to snatch the last jar for my friend.

This was the first time I had consciously stolen anything. But at the moment I did not question my act. I felt no pangs of remorse.

Back at Changi, I found my officer friend pacing up and down, anxiously awaiting me. When I showed him the Marmite he insisted on pressing ten dollars Malayan into my hand. I had a twinge of conscience. I could justify my theft on the grounds I had done it to save a man's life. But could I accept a reward for it?

I hesitated.

"Take it," he said. "It's worth much more than that."

I needed the money. At the moment I had none. This might mean survival to me. I took it. I turned away.

The norm by which we measured things was changing.

A few days later I had a violent attack of fever. My temperature went to 106. Again I was delirious, as on the *Setia Berganti*. I remember only vaguely the British medical officer drenching me with water in a desperate effort to cool my burning body.

My illness was diagnosed as malignant tertian malaria, grave enough to warrant my admittance to the Changi hospital which already was overflowing with patients.

Atabrine was not available; there was no quinine; so I literally had to sweat it out. This was but the beginning of a long series of illnesses.

When I left the hospital and returned to the Argylls, a new problem plagued me: no longer could I stomach the daily ration of rice. Attempts to flavor it with boiled leaves of hibiscus helped little.

One afternoon while I was grinding rice grains for my cereal next morning, I felt an acute stabbing pain in the abdomen.

Examination revealed that in addition to the malaria I was also supporting a colony of intestinal worms at my own expense.

The doctor dealt with them, then broke the news that my appendix appeared twisted and inflamed and had to come out.

The hospital was on an upper floor of one of the barracks buildings, open to the elements except for a bamboo screen. Two orderlies stretched me out on an old kitchen table, while the doctors prepared to operate by the fitful light of a kerosene storm lantern. The orderlies laid a pad over my mouth, sprinkled a few drops of ether on it, and off I went into dreamland.

Within a day or two I began to feel much better. I thought the time had come to speed my recuperation by adding some canned foods to my diet. For five dollars out of my ten— exactly half of my worldly goods—I was able to buy one can of Campbell's Tomato Soup. I ate it straight from the can, savoring each spoonful, and rolling it around and around my tongue before swallowing it. I don't think anything has ever tasted more delicious since.

On my return from the hospital, I noticed an upsurge of religion.

As disease spread, as spirits became depressed, as hopes first rose, then died and men had nothing to which they could look forward, they sought aid from beyond themselves.

Church services were allowed by the Japanese. They were held in the open and were well attended. But I was not interested in going. Men I knew to have no particular religious ties went regularly, listened attentively, sang hymns lustily, prayed fervently, and read their Bibles. For most, religion was an attempt to find a quick and easy answer, a release from their fears.

As human resources failed, men turned to God and said in effect,

"Look, Old Boy, I'm in trouble. I'll speak well of you if you'll get me out of it."

Churchgoing for many thus became a kind of insurance policy to protect them from personal suffering; religion a thing of formulas, ceremonials, and easy answers. They believed that if they cajoled God properly He could be persuaded to rescue them from the miseries of their present existence. They prayed for food, for freedom, or to be spared from death.

The Bible they viewed as having magic properties; to the man who could find the right key, all would be revealed. One group assured me with absolute certainty that they knew the end of the war was at hand. When I asked them for proof they told me they had found it in the books of Daniel and Revelation. They proceeded to demonstrate mathematically how they had arrived at this conclusion. They had manipulated numbers and words from these two books in a way that seemed convincing enough to them.

The dominant motivation for such wholesale embracing of religion was not love and faith, but fear: fear of the unknown, fear of suffering, fear of the terror by night, fear of death itself, fear that made for division rather than for community.

The Argylls were to leave for upcountry. It was no "borehole" rumor this time—the orders had been seen. The exact destination was not specified. It was thought to be somewhere in northern Malaya, or possibly Thailand.

I was still weak but my friends thought it would be wise if I went along; they surmised there ought to be a better food supply in the north, and also more opportunity for making an escape as we would be nearer Burma. I concurred. Packing was a simple business; I had only to wrap up my blanket, a pair of shorts, two tin cans, and a toothbrush.

Before leaving on our march to the railroad station, we were gathered together to hear an inspirational lecture by an

English-speaking Japanese officer. He began with a long political preamble, reminding us that a new era was coming into being, one reflecting the wisdom and benevolence of the mighty Japanese Emperor, the greatest ruler ever known. He explained that everyone would benefit from the new justice, and assured us that in the place where we were going we would have nothing to fear.

The officer extolled the glories of the prison camp that had been prepared for us. His phrases sounded like advertising copy for a health resort. Here, said he, we would find not only pleasant quarters and the finest of food; there would be splendid facilities for recreation and the best of care in modern hospitals for those who had the misfortune to fall ill.

We had had enough experience with the promises of our captors not to trust them. At the same time we hoped that we would find conditions a little better. In any event we would be in the countryside where fruit and vegetables ought to be more plentiful.

We were each given two balls of cooked rice, allowed to fill our water bottles, and then we started for the station, where for the first time in many weeks we were again among other people. Malays and Chinese were waiting in crowds for trains to take them away from Singapore. But we were heavily guarded and forbidden to speak to them.

Our train was shunted in. We were shoved into small, stifling metal boxcars and the doors were barred after us. Most of us remained standing. There was not enough room to sit properly, much less lie down.

The train moved out of Singapore Island across the Causeway which the Japanese, in the meantime, had repaired. Through the slits in the cars we could see the bomb craters, the twisted and shattered equipment, the burned-out trucks, all bitter memorials to the devastation of war. With a twinge, the memory of our march onto the island came back to me. It had been only four months ago—yet how much had happened in that short time!

Malays, Tamils, and Chinese, sad and sullen, stared at the train as we passed. On one of the rare occasions when we were allowed out of the cars to relieve ourselves I had the chance to speak to a Tamil who had been foreman on a rubber estate. I asked him how things were.

"Oh, bad, sir, terribly bad," he replied. "And they are getting worse."

The train went on, up into northern Malaya. At any moment we expected to reach the site of our new health camp. But the train kept going, on into Thailand. After four days and four nights locked in those cramped little cars, we reached our destination—a camp called Banpong.

We weren't hoping for much, but Banpong failed even our dimmest expectations. It was nothing but a small clearing stacked with bamboo and atap palm. If there was to be any camp at all, we would have to make it for ourselves.

Not one of the promised improvements ever materialized. Nothing was offered in the way of recreation. The only hospital was a hut which we so designated. We never saw any of the fresh fruits or vegetables which we had envisioned. We had no bedding of any kind. Latrines were open pits. For bathing we had the river. We hoarded our bits of soap for shaving, and washed ourselves with gravel or wood ash from the cookhouse fires and dried ourselves with jungle leaves.

Banpong was a step down from Changi. Our rations were the same, a small portion of rice of poor quality, in spite of the fact that our regime soon changed to hard labor. We were sent out daily on work parties to hack away at the jungle, clearing ground for other camps such as this one.

Since this was a small camp, the Japanese were right on top of us at all times, breathing down our necks. We had no privacy. There was no chance of escape. We looked out at that thickness of jungle and knew that a thousand miles of it still separated us from freedom.

Our lifesaver was the wireless. We had smuggled in a miniature set built into the bottom of a water canteen. For this we were indebted to technicians of the Royal Corps of Signals. When Singapore fell they dismantled their large receiving sets, took the parts and made up a number of little ones. Some of these found their way into the possession of prisoners at Changi.

With this set we had more news of the progress of the war than at any time before or afterward. But listening to the news was punishable by death, as we were frequently reminded. At a nearby camp five men were surprised while listening and promptly kicked to death. This punishment was ordered by a young Japanese officer who spoke English with a clear American accent. He was a graduate of Columbia University.

Most of us were never permitted to know the hiding place of the set, lest we disclose it under torture. It made its appearance at a new location every night. The prisoners kept a close watch against approaching guards. This wireless was to follow us through many camps. Its last hiding place was in an oven. But I never knew where it was concealed at Banpong.

One difficult problem was getting the power to operate it. This was supplied for a time by a fellow prisoner who had been pressed into service to drive a truck for the Japanese. Every night when he finished work he would take the battery out of his truck, hoist it onto his shoulder, and blandly carry it into camp in full sight of everyone.

One night a sentry challenged him as he was passing the guardhouse.

"Bagero!" the sentry shouted. "Where are you going with that?"

The truck driver regarded him with sleepy, innocent eyes.

"Can't you see that it's a wet night?" he said. "This battery is delicate and easily injured by dampness. Therefore, I am taking it to my bed to keep it dry."

The sentry beamed and gave him a pack of cigarettes for his faithful devotion to the Emperor.

We could take little cheer, however, from the news of the war when we did hear it. Rommel was about to take over in North Africa. The Russians were being pushed back; Moscow was in danger. The cities of Great Britain were being pitilessly bombed. The Japanese were still masters in the Pacific.

In spite of these dour tidings, the same old rash of over-optimistic "bore-hole" rumors started up again. Some of the officers, foreseeing the devastating effect on morale when these rumors proved to be false, did their best to counteract their impact. We spent evenings making the rounds of the huts, giving long-range analyses of the war, its causes and consequences and the probabilities for the eventual outcome. Whether or not these talks did any good was difficult to tell.

The officers spared no effort to bolster sagging morale. We routed out all conceivable talent for Saturday night vaudevilles. I made my contribution by singing some Scottish student songs, "As Through the Streets" and "A Lum Hat Wantin' a Croon." I cannot pretend that my efforts were warmly received. This was the first time I had ever sung in public. It was also the last.

All in all, these attempts at diversion and entertainment were something less than successful. Apathy and listlessness settled over Banpong like a miasmic fog. Morale was low and sinking steadily. We were on the long, slow slide.

CHAPTER 4

The Valley of Death

IN SEPTEMBER THE ORDER CAME FOR US TO move again. We were to be transferred to another area, somewhere farther north.

I had not recovered from the effects of my operation; I still had intermittent attacks of malarial fever. Now something new had been added to my collection. At Banpong I had contracted amoebic dysentery.

This time there was no train. We were to march to the next camp, carrying our cooking utensils and our tools, which meant that we were loaded to capacity.

I have often thought about that march and the hidden resources of the human mechanism it disclosed. My legs moved of their own accord, as though they had no relation to me, yet I plodded along, almost able to keep up with the column.

The sun rose in the sky and its heat intensifed our thirst. We walked past endless rice paddies. There, within reach, were enticing pools of muddy water. We had but to lean down, scoop it up with our hands, and drink; but to do so would be to invite death by cholera or typhoid.

The sun reached its zenith and began its descent. The blaze lessened; but now our bones ached with weariness. In spite of their best efforts, some of the men fell behind.

Twilight came. The guards who were traveling by truck were sent to round up the stragglers. They shouted insults which we did not hear and rained blows on us which we did not feel.

Camp that night was no more than a place to sit on the bare ground. For our supper, we were handed a cup of water and a ball of cold rice. We stretched out where we were and slept.

The guards routed us out early for the last lap of our journey, marching us past a village called Kanburi to the bank of a wide, muddy river that bustled with activity. Native craft, propelled by poles or outboard motors, were busily ferrying supplies from one bank to the other. No one knew the name of the river. We hadn't a clue at that time that this was the River Kwai, and that we were near the spot where we would be forced to build the hated bridge.

Open wooden barges waited by the river's edge. The guards herded us aboard, until our entire contingent—all two hundred and fifty of us—were jammed into four of them. A ridiculously little motor launch appeared and began to tow us. For several hours we stood unprotected in the sun while the sputtering launch pulled its heavy load slowly upstream against the current some two and a half miles to Chungkai.

I staggered up the muddy bank and had my first glimpse of our new camp. Nearby, I saw loose stacks of cut bamboo, other loose stacks of atap grass, and a scraggly grass hut, which I took to be the guardhouse. Beyond, wherever I looked, was the jungle—powerful, heavy, dark and green, threatening and confining.

I sat down to rest. Above me I could see the fronds of the bamboo forming a lacework pattern against the sky. A tree rat scampered along a bowing branch, paused, sniffed, and scampered on. A tiny delicate bird hovered busily for a little by a trembling leaf, then darted quickly to another tree on its quest for insects. A monkey chattered angrily, scratched itself, and swung off into the trees.

I was not allowed to rest for long. The guards came up
and we were put to work, building our own barracks Japanese
style. These were long, narrow huts of bamboo, roofed with
atap palm, with sleeping platforms made of split bamboo rising
just above the mud and extending down either side. A hut
would hold about two hundred men. Each man had to himself a space about six feet long and two feet wide—roughly the
room of a narrow grave.

We were to push the jungle back for a time, clearing an area
about three quarters of a mile long by half a mile wide.

Between the huts was earth—trampled earth, the dark
brown color of mud in the wet season, the light brown color
of dust when it was dry. In the wet season everything we
touched oozed mud. The dust in the dry season caked our
skins, stung our eyes, and choked our throats.

We had not been long at Chungkai when we found out why
we were here and why the camp existed. We learned it piece
by piece from what we saw, from "bore-hole" rumors, and
from remarks dropped by the guards. The more we learned,
the greater grew our foreboding.

We prisoners of war, in violation of all international cove-
nants, were to be used to build a railroad for the Japanese
Army. Field Marshal Juichi Terauchi of the Japanese Southern
Army had formally filed the request for our services and Tojo
himself approved it.

The enemy were planning to go on through Burma and
to invade India. But since their existing supply line was by
sea and therefore vulnerable to submarine attack, they
wanted a substitute route overland. The Japanese could
take advantage of two rail lines already in operation—one
running from Singapore to Bangkok and one in Burma between Rangoon and Ye. All that was needed to join the two
lines was to cut a railroad through jungle and hills running
from Banpong up along the River Kwai and thence through

the Three Pagodas Pass to connect with the Burma line north of Ye on the way to Moulmein.

This railroad was to be several hundred miles in length. When the Japanese engineers made their first calculations, they estimated that it would take five or six years to complete it. Once they received the go-ahead to use prisoners, they cut the projected time to eighteen months.

The building of the railroad was scheduled to commence in June, 1942. But for reasons which we never knew, construction did not get under way until almost November. In spite of this bad start, the target date for completion to fit in with the Japanese invasion timetable remained the same. An undertaking that appeared impossible to bring off in eighteen months thus had to be compressed into twelve. No one seemed quite sure how the schedule was to be met. The Japanese relieved their apprehensions by bawling and shouting which only compounded confusion with confusion. The prisoners bore the brunt of their wrath.

To get the job done, the Japanese had human flesh, but flesh was cheap. Later, there was an even more plentiful supply—Burmese, Thais, Malayans, Chinese, Tamils, and Javanese—more than sixty thousand of them, all beaten, starved, overworked, and thrown carelessly on that human rubbish heap, the Railroad of Death.

Thus began the most grueling phase of our captivity. Every morning as soon as dawn streaked the sky—at five thirty or six o'clock—we were marched from Chungkai to work at hacking out the route for the railroad. We were not marched back until late at night. Sometimes, if there was a job to be finished, we were kept working far into the early hours of the next morning.

We did this seven days a week. We lost all consciousness of time. Was it Tuesday, the fourth, or Friday, the seventeenth? Who could say? And who cared? One gray day succeeded another. Misery, despair, and death were our constant companions.

We cut down bamboo and cleared the jungle. But most of all we dug earth, carried it in boxes or baskets, dumped it on the rising railroad bed—and dug more earth.

Except for our G-strings, we worked naked and barefoot in heat which reached one hundred and twenty degrees. Our bodies were stung by gnats and insects, our feet cut and bruised by sharp stones.

The monsoons came early that year and with them a new adversary. We worked and lived in a world of wetness. One day's labor was washed away by the floods of the next. Torrents strewed rocks in our path. We understood then how unfortunate was the location of our camp at the juncture of the Kwai and the Mea Klong. Both rivers overflowed, and left us living on a raft of mud nearly up to our sleeping platforms.

Toward spring of 1943 the Japanese grew increasingly nervous that the railroad wouldn't be finished on time, and increasingly vented their anxiety on us.

Somewhere the guards had picked up the word "Speedo." They stood over us with their nasty staves of bamboo yelling "Speedo! Speedo!" until "Speedo" rang in our ears and haunted our sleep. We nicknamed the project "Operation Speedo."

When we did not move fast enough to suit them—which was most of the time—they beat us. Many no longer had the heart to endure such beatings. They slid to the ground and died.

Our work parties moved on into the hills. The route had to be dug and blasted now from solid rock. The job became harder and much more dangerous. In any undertaking so arduous there were bound to be accidents. But our overseers multiplied them by causing many unnecessary injuries and deaths because they did not care.

A guard, enraged over some trifle, would shriek a curse,

then hurl a hammer at a prisoner's head. A Japanese engineer carefully instructed two prisoners in making ready a dynamite charge. Then, while they were carrying out his instructions, he touched off the charge and blew up the P.O.W.'s. A boulder was carelessly pushed from a ledge, crushing a group of workers clearly visible below. The white of the limestone was stained red with blood.

Everywhere men collapsed in their tracks, from thirst, exhaustion, disease, and starvation. But death did not work fast enough to suit the Japanese, so they tried to hasten it.

The bridge over the River Kwai, an important link in the rail system, was built in the late spring of 1943.

Since the Japanese had no steel to spare and no heavy construction equipment, the bridge was built by hand labor—our labor. Several hundred yards in length and about three stories above the water, it was a sizable engineering job, but one that was primitive by modern standards.

Heavy square beams of teak were floated out into the river by work parties. The beams were then tilted upright and driven into the riverbed by hand-operated pile drivers. They were held in place by crossbeams. Other sections, also held together by crossbeams, were erected on top of them until the bridge rose to the level of the track.

Much has been made of the building of the bridge, but it was, in fact, a relatively minor episode in "Operation Speedo." Construction was finished in less than two months, but it took a year to build the railroad.

As officers, we had consented to supervise our men. But the time came when we were ordered to work alongside them for the glory of the Emperor and to earn our rice. This was a violation of international law which stipulated that officers were not to perform manual labor.

We refused.

"You'll be killed if you don't," declared the Japanese.

Our reply was,

"All right, go ahead—kill us."

We awaited their next move; it was not long in coming. All ranks were ordered on parade. Officers were lined up on one side. Opposite us were the "other ranks." The Japanese machine gunners "rammed one up the spout" and trained their sights on our men.

"Now will you work?" the Japanese asked us once again. This time we could only answer "Yes."

In Pierre Boulle's book *The Bridge over the River Kwai* and the film which was based on it, the impression was given that British officers not only took part in building the bridge willingly, but finished it in record time to demonstrate to the enemy their superior efficiency. This was an entertaining story. But I am writing a factual account, and in justice to these men—living and dead—who worked on that bridge, I must make it clear that we never did so willingly. We worked at bayonet point and under the bamboo lash, taking any risk to sabotage the operation whenever the opportunity arose.

All these jobs were done by men who worked from Chungkai; but this camp was also the base for at least twenty-six smaller camps strung out westward along the river and the railroad for several hundred miles to the Three Pagodas Pass near the Burmese border. At the first Chungkai was a busy staging area, a mustering point for materials and fresh men; at the last, a fetid hospital camp where the broken returned to die.

The crowded huts grew to forty. They housed nearly eight thousand at the peak, a battered population, but one that was ever-shifting, ever-changing. Batches of new P.O.W.'s arriving from Malaya replaced old hands as they were marched off to other camps farther upcountry. Friends came and went, appeared briefly and disappeared. A few we saw months later; many we saw no more. A thousand left us to work on some unnamed project and were never heard from. Smaller groups vanished often, leaving no trace. Now and then I recognized among new arrivals the face of a former acquaintance. He would be gone before I could greet him. We lived in a constant state of flux, never knowing what the next day held for us or for our fellows.

We were being slowly starved.

Our work was heavy, but our rations were light. Our diet was rice—nothing but rice—three times a day—and rice of the very poorest quality, the sweepings from the godowns. Much as we hated it, rice might have kept us going had there been enough of it. The most ever allotted officially was four hundred and twenty grams a day. This figure was purely hypothetical, however, for so many Japanese quartermasters dipped into the supply along the line that far less than that was left by the time the rice reached us.

Rations were issued on the basis of heads counted for work; no rice whatever was allowed for the sick. It appeared to be the fixed policy of the Nipponese High Command to write them off as quickly as possible and to waste no rice on them while doing it.

After a few months these scanty rations were further reduced, to provide, so we were told, better sustenance for the workers back in Japan. One can imagine that this made us very happy.

We thought much of escape, but escape was next to impossible. It was fairly easy to break through the flimsy twelve-foot bamboo fence. Guards were stationed at several points around the perimeter of the camp; others patrolled at regular intervals. They could be eluded. But if a man broke through where was he to go?

A thousand miles of jungle was the strongest fence that could surround any camp. To be caught outside meant death—immediate death at the hands of violent guards or slow death by starvation. We were not deterred by the wild animals or by the multitude of poisonous snakes in which the jungle abounded (I'd had a cobra crawl over my arm and thought nothing of it). It was the jungle itself, impersonal, menacing, that restrained us. More actively hostile were the natives—for the P.O.W. had a price on his head and the Japanese had set the price high. Of those who attempted escape there is no record of any surviving.

Four of our fellows proved how slight the chances were. They slipped through the bamboo enclosure only to be reported by natives, captured and brought back. We next saw them pegged to the ground in front of the guardhouse. The Japanese made a point of letting us know they had been tried and sentenced.

At dawn we reported as usual for work parade, knowing full well what was happening at that very moment. A ragged volley of rifle fire rang out; a short silence followed; then, one by one, four single shots from a pistol.

Our friends had made good their escape—in the only way they could.

The same fate might have been mine. Jack Hyslop and I had long plotted an escape. But when the hour came, I had one of my recurrent attacks of malaria and could not join him. Jack went anyway. But his native contacts whom he was to meet outside failed to appear as stipulated and Jack returned before he was missed.

The only purpose in breaking through the fence, therefore, was to trade on the black market with the local Thais or to forage for fruits or plants that could be used as substitutes for medicines. The villages were tiny—collections of no more than six or seven huts scattered along the Kwai not far from camp. Here the Thais cultivated their rice paddies or fished in the river.

The P.O.W.'s had an occasional penknife, fountain pen, or remnants of clothing—a pair of shorts or a shirt. These items were prized by the Thais and brought high prices. From time to time enterprising traders turned up, traveling along the river, with canned milk and native medicines for sale.

Lime and banana trees, and—more rarely—red chili peppers grew in a semi-wild state at the edge of the villages. We bartered for these, or, when occasion permitted, helped ourselves.

Such expeditions were always dangerous.

More men came pouring into camp—more men to dig earth —more men to die.

Death called to us from every direction. It was in the air we breathed—it was the chief topic of our conversation. The rhythm of death obsessed us with its beat—a beat so regular, so pervasive, so inescapable that it made Chungkai a place of shadows in the dark valley.

Dying was easy. When our desires are thwarted and life becomes too much for us, it is easy to reject life and the pain it brings, easier to die than to live. It is an easy thing to adopt a philosophy of despair: to say, "I mean nothing; there is nothing; nothing matters; I live only to die."

Those who decided they had no further reason for living, pulled down the shades and quietly expired. I knew a man who had amoebic dysentery. Compared to the rest of us, he was in good condition. But he convinced himself that he could not possibly survive and he did not. An Allied naval lieutenant reached the point where he could no longer endure his misery and tried to commit suicide. He did not succeed in his attempt, but died shortly afterward with nothing wrong with him; he died from failure of his will to live.

These were the day-to-day cases of death retail. At times we were also brought face to face with death wholesale.

On one occasion a whole string of barges came floating downriver to our camp. Their cargo consisted of corpses—the bodies of prisoners from upcountry. They were no more than skeletons covered with skin.

Without warning, cholera struck. All around us, on the job, in the huts, men suddenly became violently sick. They were carried away to the isolation area and we knew we would never see them again. So many died that the dead weren't even counted.

Cholera victims weren't buried in pits as were those who died daily; they were burned. Details were assigned to drag the bodies to the riverbank. On great blazing pyres were thrown the remains of men who had once been husbands, sons, lovers, friends. While the flames crackled around them in the shimmering heat they would turn, kick, bend, and reach, then rise in a macabre dance—their eerie dance of farewell.

As conditions steadily worsened, as starvation, exhaustion, and disease took an ever-growing toll, the atmosphere in which we lived was increasingly poisoned by selfishness, hatred, and fear. We were slipping rapidly down the scale of degradation.

In Changi the patterns of army life had sustained us. We had huddled together because of our fears, believing there was safety in numbers. We had still shown some consideration for one another.

Now that was gone, swept away. Existence had become so miserable, the odds so heavy against us, that nothing mattered except to survive. We lived by the rule of the jungle.

"red in tooth and claw"—the evolutionary law of the survival of the fittest. It was a case of "I look out for myself and to hell with everyone else."

This became our norm. We called it "The Ladder Club." Its motto was "I've got the ladder up, Jack. I'm all right." The weak were trampled underfoot, the sick ignored or resented, the dead forgotten.

When a man lay dying we had no word of mercy. When he cried for our help, we averted our heads. Men cursed the Japanese, their neighbors, themselves, and God. Cursing became such an obsession that they constructed whole sentences in which every word was a curse.

Everyone was his own keeper. It was free enterprise at its worst, with all the restraints of morality gone.

Our captors had promised to reduce us to a level "lower than any coolie in Asia." They were succeeding all too well.

Although we lived by the law of the jungle, the strongest among us still died, and the most selfish, the most self-sufficient, the wiliest and cleverest, perished with the weak.

Little acts of meanness, suspicion, and favoritism permeated our daily lives. Even the drawing of our meager ration was a humiliating experience. To get our meals we formed a line in our huts. Our server would dip his can into the rice bucket and dump its contents on our mess tins. Another server would ladle out a watery stew of green leaves.

I always watched warily when my turn came. I knew the servers would give me short measure so they would have more for themselves and for their chums. Yet I dared not protest or next mealtime I'd draw ever shorter measure. I knew this— and I knew that they knew that I knew. I hated them for knowing. And I hated myself for hating them.

We mistrusted not only the ones we could see, but also the ones we could not see. How much were the helpers in the cookhouse holding back? How much were they stealing for themselves? Suspicion gripped us.

But there were depths below depths to which some, discarding the last pretense of self-respect, yet descended.

The minute roll call was over in the evening there would be a rush to the Japanese cookhouse. The cooks would bring out swill pails and set them on the ground. Then they would stand back, fold their arms, and look on with self-satisfied smiles while prisoners pushed, kicked, and shoved one another out of the way as they fought for scraps from the enemy table.

One evening this too familiar scene was taking place as I passed by. A wretch broke away and stumbled toward me. In his hand he clutched a soggy mess of rice and stew. Bits of gravy dripped through his fingers. He had turned his back on the others, lest they should see what he had and be tempted to rob him. A wolfish leer contorted his face as he craftily licked at his spoils. He considered himself lucky.

"Rather than do that," I thought to myself, "I'd die!"

He passed me at a kind of trot, like an animal going to his lair, except that an animal would have had more dignity.

It was common practice to steal from each other.

A Malayan rubber planter named Iain Stewart, whom I had known in Singapore, turned up in Chungkai. He was pleased at finding someone he knew. The next day when I saw him again he was utterly disconsolate.

"What's wrong, Iain?" I inquired.

He could hardly speak.

"My pack's been taken," he said at last. "Some lousy bastard snatched it right from under my head last night. I've lost every bloody thing I had in the world—my fiancée's photograph, my knife, pen, notebook—the things I've hung on to all the way. But what hurts worse is to be robbed by your own kind."

"Did you shout?"

"Yes, I shouted. But no one lifted a finger. I never thought I'd see the day when a thing like this could happen."

Overcome with emotion, he removed his steel-rimmed glasses and wiped them on the strip of canvas that served to cover his loins.

"At least you still have those," I said, trying to cheer him up a bit.

"Yes, I'd be as blind as a bat without them and that would have been blinking awful, wouldn't it? I stuck them in a piece of bamboo at the foot of my sleeping platform so I wouldn't roll on them."

"Have you reported this?"

"Oh, yes. I went straight off to see the British colonel. Nothing can be done about it. Goes on all the time. We can't control it among ourselves, and the Nips don't give a damn. In fact, the more depraved we become, the more it pleases them."

"How they must be gloating over us! The white man and his civilization! What a pompous fraud!"

"Damnable, isn't it?" said Iain as he adjusted his glasses.

"Yes, damnable."

Even more damnable than those who stole from the living were the human jackals who lurked about, waiting to rob the dead. Most of the prisoners left this world picked as clean as Iain. The jackals were not above snatching their last few rags. But what lured them was the hope that they might find a watch, a ring, a knife, a pen, or even a pound note stitched into a loincloth that had been overlooked.

This ghoulish activity characterized our general attitude toward the dead. We could see only one end and that end was death. Death was never far from our thoughts.

We had no church, no chaplains, no services. If there were men who kept faith alive in their hearts they gave no sign. This was not surprising. At Changi, many had turned to religion as a crutch. But the crutch had not supported them; so they had thrown it away. Many had prayed, but only for themselves. Nothing happened. They had sought personal miracles from the Bible—and none had come. They had appealed to God as an expedient. But God apparently had refused to be treated as one.

We had long since resigned ourselves to being derelicts. We were the forsaken men—forsaken by our families, by our friends, by our government. Now even God had left us.

Hate, for some, was the only motivation for living. We hated the Japanese. We would willingly have torn them limb from limb, flesh from flesh, had they fallen into our hands. In time even hate died, giving way to numb, black despair.

One hot afternoon while we were digging to make a flat foundation for the railroad bed, our guards moved away for a minute. Our detail had a chance for a brief pause; we stood there mopping our foreheads, slapping at insects, or leaning on our shovels.

"Have you ever thought," a workmate next to me said suddenly, "how deliberately we choose death?" I told him it hadn't occurred to me. "From quite early in life we rush to throw in our lot with it," he went on. "Our education prepares us for it. We're taught that it's manly and heroic to die; the finest thing that can happen to us is to have our names preserved on a bronze plaque."

He wiped his forehead with his arm to keep the sweat from running into his eyes.

"Now women—God bless 'em—have more sense. They choose life—and they fight like hell for it—for the life they carry in their wombs and the children they have borne. Why can't we see things the way they do?"

He gazed out over the impenetrable green mass that separated us from the world and the lives we had known.

"I had a woman once. She loved me. In fact, she was fair crazy about me. When I was called up I went round to see her to tell her it was all over, thank you very much. She couldn't believe what I said to her, so I had to tell her all over again: 'It's finished, washed up, kaput,' I said. 'There's a war on or going to be very soon and I'm off to it. Love and war don't belong together and I don't want you grieving, so that's that.' I can never forget the pain in her eyes; God, she was lovely— lovelier even than she had been before, now that I was leaving her, with the pain showing in her eyes and all.

"Before I went away she came to say good-by, with the pain still there. She said she wanted me to have a book and she handed it to me. I looked at the name on it. It was called *The Importance of Living.* Bloody rummy, wasn't it?" He sighed. "What a fool I was!"

Then he went on to recite something like this—a poem he had either made up or memorized:

> *"I looked within your eyes*
> *and saw the pain you felt*
> *pain that was for me*
> *because I did not understand*
> *why you gave so much*
> *nor why you tried to cross the chasm*
> *that separated me from you.*
>
> *"We had touched, my love,*
> *that we had, flesh to flesh,*
> *but I had never met you*
> *and you were hurt*
> *yet though you were hurt*
> *you waited—*
> *and then I came to tell you*

I was going away,
with a flip 'Good-by'
not caring, not caring for you
with the pain-struck eyes.

"And I went, went to the battle
that called me from you,
called me from love,
called me from happiness,
called me to where the bloody gutters
run with life,
life that once had danced and laughed
.and dared to hope—
and there's no return."

When he had finished he fell silent. This was one of those times when silence is the only bond of understanding. I was silent too.

The Japanese guard came back. We picked up our shovels and resumed digging.

For days afterward I looked for my workmate—but I never saw him again.

So far I had been able to stay out of the Death House. In spite of my dysentery and bouts of malaria, I kept on my feet.

One day I had a sore throat. I borrowed a mirror. There was a great yellow-white patch of blood-flecked phlegm. It was a nuisance, but I didn't pay much attention to it; we couldn't concern ourselves too greatly over minor ailments.

Every now and then I tried to remove the patch. Eventually I succeeded and forgot about it, believing that I was going to be all right. I awoke one morning to find I couldn't talk properly. What was more troublesome, I could not swallow. Every time I tried to take a drink, the water came gushing back through my nose.

I reported to an examining medical officer, a doctor from Glasgow. He found my attempts to speak to him amusing—more so than I did—and he responded by mimicking me.

By this time I had a pretty good idea what was wrong with me. The blood-flecked patch was one symptom; my fallen palate another. I had diphtheria. I was sure the doctor knew too. But the pressure on him to produce workers must have been so great that he disregarded my plight. Back to work I went.

I soon noticed that I was losing sensation in my legs. They felt heavy; before long I could hardly lift one after the other.

I returned to the M.O. He diagnosed the trouble with my legs as polyneuritis, a consequence of the diphtheria. Work was impossible because I couldn't stand.

"The hospital for you," said the M.O.

This time I was headed for the Death House. However, I was so ill that I didn't much care.

But I was not prepared for what I found. The Death House had been built at one of the lowest points in the camp. The monsoon was on; the floor of the hut was a sea of mud.

And the smells: the smell of tropical ulcers eating into flesh and bone; the smell of latrines overflowed; the smell of dirty men, untended men, sick men, of humanity rotting, humanity gone sour. Worst of all was the sweet, evil smell of bedbugs by the millions, crawling over us to steal the little flesh that still clung to our bones.

Men lay in rows head to feet. One of the worst features in this jam of humanity was the loneliness; one never knew one's neighbor. Everyone was crowded together, but there was no blethering, no communion, no fellowship.

On my first day in the Death House I passed the time watching the man whose head was at my feet. I wondered whence he had come, what his name was. He scarcely moved. Suddenly he jerked up into a sitting position, twitched, fell back, and lay there. Flies clustered on his nose and mouth. Then I knew that he was dead.

The swarming flies struck me as obscene. I leaned down and tried to wave them away from him. I shouted for the orderlies. It was a long time before they came. Poor chaps. The living were their first concern. What could they do in the face of such suffering?

Once, as two men passed my sleeping platform, I overheard a scrap of their conversation.

"You know," one was saying to the other, "I never could believe that nonsense the parsons talk, about there being a hell. There ain't one—that any thinking man can be sure of. It's all superstition, aimed at keeping the working classes under control so they won't rebel against the government and the rich. It's a bloody lie, that's what it is."

"Bloody lie be damned!" replied the other. "We're all dead and this is hell. If you don't believe it, look around you."

The days went by; I grew more frail. I was no longer hungry. I had passed that stage. I did not suffer. My body was beyond pain. Still I continued to live.

Since I had no way of looking at myself I was unaware of the change in me. I was lying there in a half-stupor, watching the pattern the light made through the ragged atap palm, when I recognized a familiar figure. It was my old shipmate Edward Hooper, the skipper of the *Setia Berganti*. He must have been recently arrived at Chungkai and had come to the Death House looking for me.

Slowly he moved along between the sleeping platforms. I called to him. But it was as in a dream where you cry out and can make no sound.

He had reached the end of the hut. He had not seen me. He turned and started to leave. I was able to catch the attention of an orderly who ran after him, stopped him at the door, and brought him back.

Hooper stared at me. He showed no sign of recognition. I plucked at his wrist and he bent over. When he was close enough to hear, I muttered my name.

"Good God! You can't be Rosie!" he exclaimed with shock and disbelief.

On the prahu, when he had given me my nickname, I was a good two hundred pounds of energetic flesh on a solid six-foot-two frame.

We chatted a while—or rather he chatted—and I nodded or shook my head, and then he left.

I asked for a mirror. I did not recognize myself. Haunting, sunken eyes stared out at me above a beard. Waxy skin stretched over protruding bones. The swelling at my ankles, the edema caused by beriberi, was the only fleshy place on me.

The last shreds of my numbed sensibilities rebelled against my surroundings—against the bedbugs, the lice, the stenches, the blood-mucous-excrement-stained sleeping platforms, the dying and the dead bedmates, the victory of corruption.

This was the lowest level of life. The doorway to death was no noble stepping-off place—but a sordid snuffing-out place, a "not-with-a-bang-but-with-a-whimper" sort of place.

A few nights later I signaled one of the orderlies.

"For God's sake get me out of here!" I begged with as much force as I could muster.

"Can't," he said with a shrug.

"Why not?"

"No place to go."

"Come off it. There must be some place."

"No."

"How about letting me lie at the entrance? It's cleaner there —and the air's better."

"Can't. The M.O. wouldn't stand for it. You'd be in our way."

"How about the far end, then?"

"Can't. That's the morgue."

"What's wrong with the morgue?"

"Nothing. Except that's where we put the bodies."

"It's cleaner than this, isn't it?"

"Aye."

"Then move me!"

"Okay, then. If that's how you want it. You won't be in the way there."

He had an afterthought—a grisly one.

"But mind—if anyone puts a rice sack on you while you're sleeping—make a noise or move or something. We wouldn't want to bury you unintentionally."

He called down the hut to his mate.

"Hi, Bill! Here's a live one who wants to go to the morgue. Come—give a hand!"

Bill came along and between them they dragged me to the far end. There was no sleeping platform here. I had to lie on the ground. But at least the ground was dry.

As I slept that night I dreamed. I was happy with my dreams. Then my senses, struggling up from their pleasing rest, experienced anew the corrupt smells of dying flesh, of dying men.

The harsh light of dawn filtered in through the roof.

CHAPTER 5

Miracle by the River Kwai

MY GOOD FRIEND TOM RIGDEN, WHO HAD operated the escape service with me on the Indragiri River, had recently been brought to Chungkai to work on the railroad. He had been captured at Padang.

One evening Tom came to see me in the Death House. He wanted to tell me he had organized the building of a small hut which I was to have all to myself. My fate was a matter of concern only to my fellow P.O.W.'s. The Japanese had already written me off. All that I needed, therefore, was permission from the senior British medical officer to be moved.

When the M.O. in charge of our hut was making his morning rounds, I whispered to him.

"Doc—"

"Yes?"

"How about letting me out of this hole? Some friends of mine have built me a little shack. There's not much more you can do here for me, is there?"

"No, there isn't, Ernie," he said. "I only wish there were . . ."

He looked up and down the Death House, then back at me, lying on the ground in the morgue.

"The only reason for keeping you here is to isolate you from some of the healthier lads. A hut of your own would do that as well and would be a lot more comfortable for you. Tell you what—I'll ask the senior medical officer when he comes around. Okay?"

"Okay."

"You can depend on me," the M.O. replied.

I watched him continue on his rounds, pausing to chat with each of his wretched patients and to encourage them with his gentle smile.

Inside of an hour he was back with the S.M.O. They stood beside me, while the M.O. presented my case.

The S.M.O. hesitated. The M.O. continued,

"I could still look in on him every day. He's a friend of mine anyway and I always like to have a word with him. What are your views?"

At this point they both moved away a little, beyond my listening range—or so they thought. But I could hear them.

"I gather he's had a pretty rugged time of it," the S.M.O. said in a low voice.

"He's had the works," the M.O. answered. "Malaria, dysentery, beriberi, plus some queer kind of blood infection we can't identify. Oh, yes, he's also had an appendectomy. And on top of that a bad case of 'dip' which left him without the use of his legs."

"Not exactly in the pink, eh?"

"Hardly. His blood count is way down. And his pulse is very weak."

"Too bad." The S.M.O. shook his head. "The only thing left is to let him have a decent end."

He looked questioningly at the M.O.

"How's he going to look after himself? He can't walk, can he?"

"No, he can't. But I'm sure his friends will help him. It won't be for long in any case."

The S.M.O. continued to look at the M.O. Then he nodded decisively. The M.O. came back to my side.

"It's all right. You're free to go whenever you can be picked up."

I thanked him. The two men moved on.

The death sentence had been pronounced on me by experts.

I had faced death before: once in my early pilot-training days when I had crashed in a disabled plane; once when I had looked into the angry eye of a machine gun sending its bullets thudding into my shoulder; again at the time of our capture when we were all told we would be treated as spies and shot.

There were other occasions, familiar to most men who have been in action. Death, after all, is part and parcel of the soldier's trade.

This time, however, the business of dying seemed so much more matter-of-fact. Here in this prison camp it was "the done thing." The only variable, so far as I could see, was the time—when?

I tried to appraise my situation, carrying on an argument with myself:

"Doctors naturally are pessimistic. They have to be. They know they'll lose in the end. But they've made mistakes before and they'll make them again. This time I'll be the one to prove them wrong."

Reason, however, had a voice of its own. It made itself heard now:

"Why should you be so different? I'll bet others before you have said the same and yet they have died. The doctors have seen a lot of men go out—their clinical experiences have been immense. They know what they're about, don't they? What makes you think they're wrong in your case?

"Let's face it, old chum—not merely the facts but the analysis of the facts are both against you. Why not face up to it and bow out as gracefully as you can?"

I wasn't giving in. But to please my troublesome friend Reason and to quiet its nagging voice, I conceded.

"Okay. In case I should kick the bucket I'll try to leave my affairs as tidy as possible."

In my pack, which I used as a pillow, I had a pencil stub and a few pieces of paper. I propped myself up on one elbow. I held the paper against the back of my mess tin, and wrote slowly, a sentence at a time, a letter to my parents:

Dear Mum and Dad,

If one of my friends passes this on to you it will mean that I've guessed wrongly and that I'm not coming back. I'm sorry. I'd have made it if I could. When I escaped, first from Singapore and then from Sumatra, I thought I was bound to return to you safely.

Don't have any regrets. I suppose it just couldn't have been otherwise. I've enjoyed life. I'm glad I was brought up in the country with the sea at the front of the house and the hills at the back. I'm glad I had you as parents. If I seldom showed any sign of appreciation for all the love and kindness you've given me, it was because I took it too much for granted that this is the way life is. I know it isn't always that way, now. Accept a "Thank you" from me to you, please!

I've enjoyed all the things I've ever done. Even those things I should have done better.

That summer before the war was absolutely wizard. I should have spent more time with you and less time sailing. But you'll forgive me for that, I know, because you liked sailing, too.

I think there's over a hundred pounds in the bank at Innellan, another forty or so in the Hong Kong and Shanghai Bank of Singapore, and maybe the Army will chip in what pay I have coming to me.

Take it and have a good vacation in the south of England. Stay at a hotel where your breakfast will be served in bed. You'll make me happy if you do this.

There's a great deal of good about life that will never die. There's a goodness at the heart of it, I believe.

Pass on my love to my friends, and be assured of mine for you, always. Kiss Grace and Pete for me.

Bless you!

Aye yours,
Ernest.

I folded the letter to give to Tom Rigden.

I lay back on my bed of earth and looked at the scene around me. Light falling through the holes in the roof made strange patterns on the rows of bodies lying so stiffly and so quietly. It was hard to tell which were dead and which still lived.

The atmosphere of the Death House was anti-life, the atmosphere of decay, of the potential "to be," ebbing away.

"You're part of this," said Reason. "There is no escape."

Memory, however, recalled me to the sanity I had known.

Going to die, was I? I found myself resisting the whole idea. I recalled the long faces and solemn words of the doctors. With a grin I answered myself in the words of Eliza Doolittle, "Not bloody likely!"

When, for me, was not now.

"The battle between life and death goes on all the time," I said to myself. "Life has to be cherished, not let go. I have made up my mind. I am not going to surrender."

Then I asked myself, "What do I do about it?"

It was a voice other than Reason that replied,

"You could live. You could be. You could do. There's a purpose you have to fulfill. You'll become more conscious of it every day that you keep on living. There's a task for you; a responsibility that is yours and only yours."

"Good enough," I said to myself. "I'll get on with it."

That afternoon I sent word to Tom that I could leave the Death House. A little while before roll call, he came for me with two friends and a borrowed stretcher.

"Don't get ideas that from now on you're going to be the Queen of Sheba," said Tom as he jogged along. "Last time we're going to do anything like this for you. You've got to get so ruddy well that you can carry *us* when our turn comes. Right, chaps?"

"Too right it is!" the others answered. "This is his last ride in the jungle limousine. From now on it's shank's mare for Ernie!"

In contrast to the Death House, my new home, clean and neatly swept, was fresh with tangy smells of newly-cut bamboo and atap palm. My friends had made excursions to the piles by the riverbank, bringing back an armful at a time until they had enough to build my shack.

It had been added on to the wall of the hut where Tom slept, and sloped down from a height of about six feet at its peak. I was not shut off by myself. Through a door at the side, about four feet high, I could look out onto the life of the camp.

My sleeping platform was neatly made from bamboo split into narrow strips. Two rough, clean rice sacks served as a covering.

Tom looked about him admiringly.

"Why, this place is so posh," he said, "you'll soon have chaps coming here from all over the camp to see how a bloated capitalist lives!"

I thought I detected a forced note in his cheerfulness. I wondered if he had been talking to the doctors.

The stretcher-bearers picked up my wasted frame, and, while one of them supported my useless legs, laid me tenderly on the clean bed. I tried to thank them.

This seemed to embarrass Tom. He was not one for sentiment. He had knocked around a bit. A Londoner born, he had gone to sea at an early age as an apprentice to the P. & O. Steamship Company. He had been troubled with asthma, and a life at sea was the doctor's prescription for him.

He had stayed with the P. & O. until he qualified as a master mariner. Then he had started a new career ashore with the Malayan Government, serving in his spare time with the Royal Naval Volunteer Reserve.

Tom sat down on the side of my bed.

"Quite all right, chum, quite all right," he said. "You ought to find it a bit better than that stinking Death House. We thought we'd like you to enjoy yourself in comfort—for a little while, anyway."

He seemed to realize he'd made a gaff, for he added hastily,

"By the way, I scrounged an old bucket you can use as a head. I've got it outside."

"My own private bathroom and everything! Why, this is a suite at the Ritz!"

"More than the Nips will ever do for you, that's sure." Tom jumped up. "Look here, old boy. It's getting to be time for evening roll call. I'd better be going along."

At the door he said casually,

"I ran into one of your Argyll lads this morning."

"Oh, yes?"

"I said you could do with a bit of help until you got on your feet properly again. Hope you don't mind."

"That's mighty decent of you. I expect I could use an extra hand for a while."

"I should jolly well think so. Don't worry. There'll be someone along to see that you have your rice and a wash."

He went out, then poked his head back in the doorway.

"Roll call is on your side of the hut, so you'll hear everything that goes on. What I mean is, you'll hear those bloody little bastards screaming their bloody heads off. It may amuse you."

Tom was gone and I was alone in the silence, a silence that was broken presently by the sounds of bare feet thudding dully on the ground, wooden sandals clattering and clobbering, the commands of the guards, and the monosyllabic answers of the prisoners.

Then it was over and I heard the pleasing hum of many voices raised in conversation as men straggled back to their huts.

These were the sounds of life.

I stretched back gratefully on my rice sacks. I don't know how long I had been lying there in that twilight state halfway between dozing and waking when I heard a polite cough. A man was standing in the doorway. He had to bend over to look in. He was quite naked except for his clean loincloth. I could see a head of fair, thick curly hair just under the top of the door. What impressed me most was his easy, friendly smile.

"Good evening, sir," he said in his soft north-of-England voice. "I've heard you needed a hand. I wondered if you'd care to have me help you."

I could hear myself saying faintly,

"Thank you, I would. Come in."

I motioned to him to sit down beside me, explaining,

"My voice isn't as strong as it used to be."

I had a better look at him. Emaciated though he was, he had the fresh complexion of a country man. I saw that he had a fine face. There was kindness in it, and a gentle strength.

"You don't know me," he said, "but I was posted to your company."

I racked my brain.

"That's funny. I can't remember you."

"I'm not surprised. I was with the reinforcements that arrived when the battalion was in training up at Seremban."

"Did you join us there?"

"No, I didn't, sir. That's where the Corps of Military Police got their hands on me and I was removed from battalion strength. Officially, I'm a military policeman, but I still look upon myself as an Argyll."

He continued earnestly, "I did my best to get permission to join the battalion when it was in action. But it was no use. I wasn't allowed to change."

"That's the Red Caps for you," I replied. "They never have been friends of the Argylls. No wonder they wanted to hang on to you. What's your name?"

"Miller, sir."

" 'Dusty,' eh? That's what all the Millers are called, isn't it?"

"Yes, sir—the Dusty Millers—that's us."

"Well, then, I'll call you Dusty."

"Certainly, sir."

I studied him for a moment.

"Dusty, are you quite sure you want to help me?" I asked the question not knowing what to expect. His offer surprised me, for it was so different from the attitude we had come to accept as normal. It seemed aeons since I had heard anyone volunteer to help a sick man.

"I'm still pretty weak," I warned him. In order to provide him with a way to withdraw his offer I said, "There's hardly anything I can do for myself."

"Of course I want to help you," he replied with such warmth and enthusiasm that there was no doubting his sincerity. "I'm recovering from an attack of diphtheria and—"

"The old 'dip,' eh?" I broke in. "Nasty stuff. Mine wasn't diagnosed until too late. That's one reason I'm lying here like this."

Dusty's eyes reflected his sympathy.

"Guess I was lucky," he said. "I got off easily. I'm still on light work, though. I've a night job in the kitchens, so I can be with you most of the day."

"That's kind of you. I'll try not to give too much trouble."

"I'm sure you won't. Here, let me get you settled for the night. I'll fetch some hot water from the cookhouse and give you a proper wash."

Dusty returned, carrying a steaming bamboo bucket, a

basin, and some rags. He then proceeded to refresh me with the first decent wash I'd had in six weeks. It felt good to be clean again!

He was ready to do my legs. We both looked down at them. They were not a pretty sight. Skin ulcers had laced them with an ugly pattern of open sores, half-formed scabs, and dried blood.

"Mm, quite a mess, aren't they?" said Dusty. "I think I'd better wash them first. Then I'll clean out the pus."

He gave them a thorough soaking with hot water. Then he took a piece of wet rag and began pressing gently against either side of the sores. He kept looking up at me as he did so, expecting me to protest.

"Go ahead. Press as hard as you like. I can't feel a thing."

This distressed him more than if I had complained, for the absence of pain told him how far advanced my condition was.

"You have a deft touch," I said. "What did you do back in civvy street?"

"I worked with my father just outside Newcastle. He was a landscape gardener."

"A gardener, eh? Did you really like that kind of work?"

"Oh, yes. I was very happy with it. I'm one of the lucky ones."

"What's lucky about that?" I asked.

"To do what you like to do and be paid for it? That's something these days, isn't it?"

"I like gardens," I said as I watched him, admiring the skill with which he worked. "But only after someone else has done the hard part."

"Many people feel as you do," he replied. "Actually, plants and flowers are much more interesting than you'd think if you don't know them. Each has its own character. Every one is unique. But they all need the gardener's care to help them make the most of themselves and to fight off the things that would destroy them. Yes, I enjoy growing things and I like trying to understand how and why they grow."

With one knee on the ground, he was bent over, intent on making me comfortable. He considered carefully before he spoke. He was a man who thought about what he was going to say. The clearly enunciated syllables, uttered in his soft voice, made pleasing music. There was an air of natural innocence or goodness about him. I did not quite know what to make of him. I was accustomed to companions who were quick of tongue and temper. Why the devil, I thought, is he so pleased to be alive?

"Weeds," I prompted, in order to keep him talking. "Gardening to me always meant weeding when I would have much rather been doing something else."

Dusty laughed.

"When people are down on their knees weeding they think only of the weeds and never of the flowers. I like to grow flowers, not weeds. But if I'm to grow flowers, I must deal with the weeds. So I don't mind doing that."

He paused while he wrung out his rag in the basin.

"I'm looking forward to getting back to my work when all this is over. Dad isn't growing any younger and one day I'll be taking over from him."

An added note of enthusiasm came into his voice.

"There'll be a great need for gardens after the war—especially in the cities. That's something I'd like very much to do—bring greenery and flowers into brick and stone to remind people of the beauty that outlasts the ugliness of war."

He smiled happily at the prospect.

"That's fine!" I said with a touch of irony. "You make your gardens and I'll come to enjoy them."

"Fair enough," he replied.

Dusty finished treating my sores. Then he produced two lengths of cloth and wound them around my legs, pulled the rice sacks smooth beneath me, and picked up his bucket, basin, and rags.

"I've a bit more to do in the kitchen, so I'll say good-night. I'll be back in the morning with your breakfast. I'll try to bring some salt, then I can make saline dressings for your legs. Have a good night's sleep."

It was a gentle command.

Dusty bent his back and disappeared through the doorway into the gathering darkness.

True to his promise, he returned in the morning with a steaming bowl of "pap rice"—rice which had been crushed by a stone and boiled as a porridge.

He also brought salt and set about preparing the saline dressings. As he worked we talked.

"Do you really think I'm going to get better?" I asked the question bluntly. I wanted to see what he would say.

He set his basin down and stood up.

"Of course you will, sir!" he said confidently. "Why shouldn't you?"

I did not answer.

"The lads have told me how fit you were when you were with the battalion," he went on. "They said you didn't wear out easily. By the time you get back to Blighty you'll be strong. And there'll be lots to do."

I turned the conversation back to him.

"And what do you have in mind apart from gardening?"

"Oh, I've plenty. For one thing, I'm looking forward to being a family man. For another, I used to help out with youth work in my local church, and I want to do more of that. There's something satisfying about working with people—especially young people."

"What makes you think you'll be able to do any good?" I asked.

Dusty looked up with raised eyebrows.

"Why, when you work with people, there's always good to be given and good to be received. At least I've always found it so, haven't you, sir?"

I challenged this.

"I'm not sure that I have. In fact, I haven't thought much about it. Perhaps it's the way you say it is—but then again perhaps it isn't."

"Oh, it is, sir, believe me," Dusty replied feelingly.

He had finished with me and was tidying up the shack. He first sprinkled water on the dirt floor, then swept it with a broom he had made from the leafy tips of branches.

"Why don't you go off for a snooze?" I remarked. "You must be tired after your night's work. When do you sleep?"

He shrugged.

"Don't worry about me. I manage all right."

Dusty went on with his chores. I was drowsing on my rice sacks, when I heard a strange voice boom out,

"Good morning, sir! Nice place you've got. I heard you were here so I thought I'd drop around to say 'Hello.' "

It was Dennis Moore of the Royal Corps of Signals. We had met when we were both in school at Greenock. But I had not seen him again until a short time before my present illness.

Dennis—better known as Dinty—was lounging with one arm against the bamboo wall just inside the doorway, as though reluctant to come in until formally invited. His hazel eyes were merry in a wide, good-natured face.

When a man is wearing nothing more than a loincloth he can hardly be described as well-groomed. Yet that was the impression Dinty conveyed, perhaps through the neatness of his hairline mustache and his carefully brushed hair.

"A friend of mine in the Argylls happened to mention that you weren't exactly at your brightest," Dinty said lightly. "I thought I'd drop by and see if I could do anything for you."

"That's awfully good of you," I replied. "This is Dusty Miller. Dusty's my nurse—since last night."

Dusty smiled in greeting. Dinty made himself at home, squatting on his haunches, feet flat on the ground native fashion, in the middle of the floor.

"Maybe there's some way I can work with you in helping the captain get his strength back," he said to Dusty. "Is there any particular time you'd like me to look in?"

"I'm on night duty in the kitchens," Dusty answered. "If you could lend a hand then, that would be fine."

"Sure thing. I'm busy daytimes on a work detail on the railway. Actually I'm supposed to be on the job right now. But the Nips sent me for a spanner. I'm taking my time about it."

"How are you making out?" I asked.

Dinty ran his thumb along the neat line of his mustache; then he replied,

"Remember what the old lady said when she sat down on her false teeth? She said, 'Oh, well, things could always be worse. It might have been my real ones.'"

He made a face, then went on,

"I may be getting a posh job soon. I was a sorting clerk in the post office back home. I hear a mountain of mail has arrived and they'll want to use my rare talents as a sorter once the Japs give the go-ahead."

He stood up.

"Must be nipping back with the spanner. Chin, chin, skipper. See you tonight."

I expected Dinty to drop in now and then, but I had no idea from his offhand manner that he intended to make me his full-time charge. Thus began a close association. No two men could have been more different. Dusty was quiet, serene, and gentle; Dinty, impulsive, full of fun, with a harum-scarum love of life. Their care and patience were successful substitutes for the medicines that were beyond my reach. No man could have asked for better nurses or for better friends. They put me on the road to recovery.

The 31st of May, 1943, dawned like any other day. It was only after Dusty had given me a wash-up and I was lying there thinking, that I remembered it was my twenty-sixth birthday. I decided not to mention it. There was no place for birthday observances here.

That evening I was surprised to see Dusty and Dinty entering together. They were singing, somewhat off key but with great spirit, "Happy Birthday."

Dinty, wearing a grin like a proud Cheshire cat, brought his hand slowly from behind his back and held out a birthday cake. It was made from boiled rice, limes, bananas, and palm sugar.

I have had tastier birthday cakes in my life, but none which meant more to me.

"Let's have a party!" I croaked, entering into their mood.

"Too right!" responded Dinty gaily. "It's all laid on!"

He went out and returned almost at once with a soot-blackened can.

"Coffee—hot and sweet!" He handed mugs around. "Coffee that some critics might say was nothing but burned rice. But I say this is coffee and I'll stand by it."

Both of them raised their mugs in salutation. Dinty gave the toast:

"Here's to your happy birthday—and to far happier ones to come!"

Their kind and spontaneous gesture of goodwill moved me deeply. For a while I was unable to respond. Finally I whispered,

"Thanks, both of you. In Blighty we'll have the biggest and fanciest birthday party anyone has ever seen. You, Dinty, can produce the dancing girls."

"Oh, I can do that, all right."

"And you, Dusty, can provide the flowers."

"That'll be right in my line."

"You can count on me for the rest."

Both answered simultaneously,

"That's a date! We'll be there."

We shook hands. We would all be there—if human wills could make it possible.

They were two rare characters—so different, yet so alike— the one, nature's gentleman, the other, a gay cavalier.

I couldn't say how or when, because it happened so slowly, but gradually sensation returned to my limbs. I started a strict regime. While I was still so weak that I could do it for only a few minutes at a time, I would sit up on the edge of my bed with my legs hanging over. I first picked up one leg and let it fall, then the other. I could encircle each thigh with my hands.

By this time Dusty's care had cleared up the worst of my tropical ulcers. His massage and my exercises helped the blood to circulate. The muscle tone returned and before long I could swing my legs from the knee.

The time came when I was able to stand on my feet by holding on to Dusty. One morning I found that with the help of a bamboo staff, I could propel myself in a clumsy, halting way as far as the door. In a matter of days I ventured outside.

As I staggered along between the huts of the camp, gaunt and bony, I must have looked like a prophet of doom. My long black beard and loincloth might well have marked me as an eremite returning from a fast in the desert.

Like Jeremiah, I could have been crying.

"My grief is beyond my healing, my heart is sick within me. . . . The harvest is past, the summer is ended, and we are not saved. . . . Is there no balm in Gilead? Is there no physician there?"

Now I had further problems to face. The amoebae thrived on my general weakness and played havoc with my insides. I never had more than half an hour's undisturbed rest without having to trot—if one could call it that—to the latrine.

I was determined, however, to do everything as though I were at the top of my strength. My skin ulcers and the beriberi were almost cured. I was convinced that in a short time I'd have the dysentery cured as well.

What I had experienced—namely, the turning to life away from death—was happening to the camp in general. We were coming through the valley. There was a movement, a stirring in our midst, a presence.

Stories of a different kind began to circulate around the camp, stories of self-sacrifice, heroism, faith, and love.

"Do you remember Angus McGillivray?" Dusty asked me late one afternoon as he made me ready for my wash.

"Indeed I do," I replied. "He was in my company. A darned good soldier, too. Yes, I know him well. As a matter of fact, I defended him at a court-martial on the charge of refusing to obey an order given him by his platoon sergeant. In my opinion he had every right to do so. It was a stupid order. Angus queried it and was immediately placed under arrest."

Dusty waited with interest as I continued my recollections.

"At the trial I put everything into the defense. Pulled out every stop in the organ. Backed every fact with reams of law."

I explained to Dusty that I had studied law while I was in the Army.

"I was doing so well that at the end of the first day Angus Macdonald, the adjutant who was prosecuting, said to me, 'You've won hands down. I'm on McGillivray's side now.'"

"Did you get an acquittal?"

"No, I didn't. The court acquitted him of the charge of disobedience, but got him on that nebulous charge of 'Conduct prejudicial to good order and military discipline.'

I've always thought it was damned bad law to have a charge as general as that on the books. Every soldier worth his salt could be convicted of it at some time or another. The adjutant admitted it was the sergeant who should have been convicted and not Angus McGillivray. And that was exactly what I told the court. Aye, he was a good soldier. He came from Lochgilphead at the top of Loch Fyne. Fine stock it was that he came from. He joined the Army because he couldn't find any work."

"Was he with the battalion long?" Dusty asked.

"For the length of his service, which must be over eight years. He was on the northwest frontier of India most of the time the battalion was fighting there. You were asking me if I knew him. Yes, I knew him all right. Why?"

"He's dead."

"Dead? How?"

For a moment Dusty could not speak. I could see that he was feeling deeply. I wondered why. He scarcely could have known McGillivray.

"It's hard to say. He was strong. In fact, he was one of those you'd expect to be the last to die. But then, I suppose he needn't have done."

"Then why did he?"

Dusty sat down on my bed.

"It has to do with Angus' mucker," he began, "who became very ill."

It was the custom among Argylls for every man to have a mucker—that is, a pal or friend with whom he shared, or "mucked in," everything he had.

"It seemed pretty certain to everyone," Dusty continued, "that the mucker's number was up. Certain, that is, to everyone but Angus. He made up his mind that his mucker shouldn't die.

"Someone had stolen his mucker's blanket. Angus gave him

his own. Every mealtime Angus would show up to draw his ration. But he wouldn't eat it. He would bring it round to give to his friend. Stood over him, he did, and made him eat it. Going hungry was hard on Angus, mind you, because he was a big man with a big frame."

While Dusty talked on I could see it all happening—Angus drawing on his strength through his will and depleting his own body to make his mucker live.

"His mates noticed that Angus had taken to slipping out of the camp at night," Dusty went on. "The nightly excursions could have only one purpose. He was visiting the Thai villages. This must have meant he had joined the black-market gang. Angus, of all people! This shocked the others, for he was known as a man of high principles."

It was possible in the camp, as men died, to come into possession of objects of some value—shirts, shorts, knives, and, occasionally, watches. The Thais would pay gladly for them in their paper money known as "bahts." A baht was worth about twenty-one cents. Or they would barter for the goods, offering medicines or duck eggs.

Although Angus' mates were of the opinion he must be trying to make a bit of money for himself, they did not hold it against him.

"Perhaps you know the end of the story," he continued. "The mucker got better. Then Angus collapsed. Just slumped down and died."

Dusty could say no more.

"And what did the docs believe to be the cause?" I asked.

"Starvation," answered Dusty, "complicated by exhaustion. He had mucked in with everything he had—even his life."

"And all for his friend!"

Dusty sat in stillness. After a while I said,

"Do you remember that verse from St. John that used to be read at memorial services for those who had died in World

War I? It went like this: 'Greater love hath no man. . . .' "

"Yes, I remember it," Dusty said, nodding. "I've always thought it one of the most beautiful passages in the New Testament: 'This is my commandment, That ye love one another as I have loved you. Greater love hath no man than this, that a man lay down his life for his friends.' "

Dusty stood without moving. Then he said,

"That's for Angus, all right."

"By some ways of reckoning," I said, "what he did might seem foolish."

"But in other ways," Dusty returned, "it makes an awful lot of sense."

He bent over my legs and went on cleansing my ulcers.

During the next few days on my visits to the latrine I heard other prisoners discussing Angus' sacrifice. The story of what he had done was spreading rapidly throughout the camp. Evidently it had fired the imagination. He had given us a shining example of the way we ought to live, even if we did not.

The incidents of which we were hearing now impressed us profoundly.

One that went the rounds soon after concerned another Argyll. He was in a work detail on the railroad.

The day's work had ended; the tools were being counted. When the party was about to be dismissed the Japanese guard declared that a shovel was missing. He insisted someone had stolen it to sell to the Thais. He strode up and down in front of the men, ranting and denouncing them for their wickedness, their stupidity, and, most unforgivable of all, their ingratitude to the Emperor.

Screaming in broken English, he demanded that the guilty one step forward to take his punishment. No one moved. The guard's rage reached new heights of violence.

"All die! All die!" he shrieked.

To show that he meant what he said, he pulled back the bolt, put the rifle to his shoulder, and looked down the sights, ready to fire at the first man he saw at the end of them.

At that moment the Argyll stepped forward, stood stiffly to attention, and said calmly,

"I did it."

The guard unleashed all his whipped-up hatred; he kicked the hapless prisoner and beat him with his fists. Still the Argyll stood rigidly at attention. The blood was streaming down his face, but he made no sound. His silence goaded the guard to an excess of rage. He seized his rifle by the barrel and lifted it high over his head. With a final howl he brought the butt down on the skull of the Argyll, who sank limply to the ground and did not move. Although it was perfectly evident that he was dead, the guard continued to beat him and stopped only when exhausted.

The men of the work detail picked up their comrade's body, shouldered their tools, and marched back to camp. When the tools were counted again at the guardhouse no shovel was missing.

As this story was retold, remarkably enough, admiration for the Argyll transcended hatred for the Japanese guard.

News of similar conduct began to reach our ears from other camps. One incident concerned an Aussie private who had been caught outside the fence while trying to obtain medicine from the Thais for his sick friends. He was summarily tried and sentenced to death.

On the morning set for his execution he marched cheerfully along between his guards to the parade ground. The Japanese were out in full force to observe the scene. The Aussie was permitted to have his commanding officer and a chaplain in attendance as witnesses. The party came to a halt. The C.O. and the chaplain were waved to one side. The Aussie was left standing alone.

Calmly, he surveyed his executioners. Then he drew a small copy of the New Testament from a pocket of his ragged shorts. He read a passage unhurriedly to himself. His lips moved but no sound came from them.

What that passage was, no one will ever know. I cannot help wondering, however, if it were not those words addressed by Jesus to his disciples in the Upper Room:

> "Let not your heart be troubled:
> Ye believe in God, believe also in me.
> In my Father's house are many mansions:
> If it were not so, I would have told you.
> I go to prepare a place for you.
> And if I go and prepare a place for you,
> I will come again, and receive you unto myself;
> That where I am, there ye may be also.
> . . . Peace I leave with you,
> My peace I give unto you:
> Not as the world giveth, give I unto you.
> Let not your heart be troubled,
> Neither let it be afraid."

He finished reading, returned his New Testament to his pocket, looked up, and saw the agitated face of his chaplain. He smiled, waved to him, and called out,

"Cheer up, Padre. It isn't as bad as all that. I'll be all right."

He nodded to his executioner as a sign that he was ready. Then he knelt down, and bent his head forward to expose his neck.

The Samurai sword flashed in the sunlight.

The examples set by such men shone like beacons.

Our regeneration—sparked by conspicuous acts of self-sacrifice—had begun while "Operation Speedo" was at its height, when work on the railroad was in its most exhausting phase and we were at the very bottom of the abyss.

At first I became conscious of the change in the camp only at second hand through what I picked up on my visits to the latrine, for I was still restricted as an invalid.

The changes in attitude toward others were most in evidence among the sick, for the able-bodied—or comparatively able-bodied—still went out every day to toil on the railroad.

But after the bridge was built, and as the railroad neared completion, the atmosphere changed. The Japanese grew less jittery. At Chungkai, those of us who were left alive enjoyed a brief respite from brutal pressure, lasting through Christmas when the camp was engulfed again by the flood of men coming back from upcountry.

That respite, brief as it was, created a climate in which our efforts to help one another and to improve our situation were able to grow and flourish.

The Japanese were getting bored; so for a time they not only permitted but encouraged our attempts to provide diversion.

During this period the Japanese also decided to pay us. Officers were to be compensated according to rank; all others according to the amount of work done.

I was pleased to hear the news, but disappointed when I learned that the sick were not to be included. It was considered an insult to the Emperor to be unable to work.

Late as the pay was in coming and meager though it was—the Japanese managed to deduct most of it for room and board—it provided another flicker of hope; now opportunities arose for replacing selfishness with a more creative way of living.

A fellow officer I scarcely knew stopped at my shack to tell me that one evening the senior British officer in charge of camp administration had called a conference of other administrative officers in his hut to effect a drastic change in camp policy.

It was first proposed that the officers agree to use part of their allowance to buy food from the canteen to give to the sick. This met with a mixed reception: some grumbled; others openly opposed it. The objections still echoed the old ways of looking at things:

"My pay is my own, isn't it? I can do with it as I please."

"We're all in a tough spot; but I need everything I can get for myself."

"When the chips are down, it's a case of 'to hell with everyone else.' Too bad, but that's the way life is."

The rejoinder was, "We sink or swim together. We ought to realize that an officer's first responsibility is to his men, and ours are in a bad way. We must share what we have with them." The opposition began to crumble. For the most part consciences had been touched. Some were still not too happy about the decision, but the ruling was accepted.

Generosity proved contagious. Once begun, this charity soon extended beyond regimental loyalties to include any man in need.

Although the pay which the "other ranks" had to share was even less than that of the officers, they, too, found ways to give expression to their impulses. For one baht a couple of duck eggs might be purchased through the canteen, which was run by the Japanese for the prisoners at exorbitant profit. A duck egg might well save a life. Sometimes a detachment arriving from another camp after a forced march would be surprised to have gifts of food pressed upon them.

It was dawning on us all—officers and "other ranks" alike —that the law of the jungle is not the law for men. We had seen for ourselves how quickly it could strip us of our humanity and reduce us to levels lower than the beasts.

Death was still with us—no doubt about that. But we were being slowly freed from its destructive grip. We were seeing for ourselves the sharp contrasts between the forces that make for life and those that make for death. Selfishness, hatred, jealousy, and greed were all anti-life. Love, self-sacrifice, mercy, and creative faith, on the other hand, were the essence of life, turning mere existence into living in its truest sense. These were the gifts of God to men.

We began to notice these forces at work around us. When we marched out into the countryside on labor details we saw them in the actions of Christian natives.

We were accustomed to being treated by the natives with indifference or contempt. Thai maidens held their noses as we passed, although perhaps they were being only practical. Sometimes we encountered yellow-robed Buddhist priests going along the road with their silver begging bowls. Our plight meant nothing to them—why should it? They were on their way to salvation by nonattachment.

But we came once to a village where the treatment we received was so different it astonished us. There was mercy in the eyes of those who rushed to the roadside to watch us go by. Before we had reached the end of their settlement they were back laden with cakes, bananas, eggs, medicines, and money which they thrust into our hands. In time we learned that this village had been converted to Christianity by missionaries, and that the Japanese, who found out about their friendly behavior, severely punished them for it.

A key figure in carrying the light of Christianity to these jungle outposts had been an elderly missionary woman who managed to continue her work during the Japanese occupation. When she was forced finally to take to the jungle, she was handed along from one group of Christians to another. The Japanese knew of her existence and were never far behind. But although they put a high price on her head, she eluded them.

These brief contacts with the outside world were helpful reminders that a saner, more human way of life still existed. No word had been said. But the message had been given.

Within the camp there were also daily inspirations. The strong and simple faith of Dusty Miller was one of them. It suggested that he had found the answer so many of us sought.

Before he went off to his work in the kitchens one evening we were having a discussion about the horrifying waste of life at Chungkai. It seemed a good time to test him with the kind of disputation which had become so familiar to me as a university student.

As he was putting fresh dressings on my tropical ulcers, I said to him,

"Dusty—do you realize that more than twenty men are dying here every day, and most of them are young?" I dragged myself up into a sitting position the better to argue with him. "Well then, doesn't it make it all the more certain that there is no meaning of any kind to be found in a situation as hopeless as this one? When you examine the facts, isn't it hard to see any point in living?"

Dusty got up from the ground where he had been kneeling, moved his basin into a corner out of the way, and looked at me with hurt surprise.

"I'm not sure I follow you. I see a lot of point in living."

I thought, "He's taking this much too calmly. He must have his doubts as I do." To test him further, I made my argument harder.

"It's quite simple. All I'm saying is that when you examine the problem of our existence, the only thing you can do is to admit, as Matthew Arnold did, that we are here on earth 'as on a darkling plain,' doomed by the processes of nature to die. Isn't that what we have to face?"

"There's more to face than that, surely," Dusty replied gently, wringing out his rag, "because there's more to life than that."

I continued,

"We may dream about love, truth, beauty, and aspiration for our own amusement, to dull the ache of existence. In fact, it's about all we can do. Actually, they're nothing but froth on the wave."

I was warming to the thrust of my logic.

"Religion and the arts are like a gramophone record we play to drown the cries of pain from the people of the world. Admittedly, they help numb the senses. But drugs can do that so much better."

Dusty looked puzzled.

"No, sir, I cannot believe that," he replied with spirit. "I don't think there *is* anything accidental about our creation. God knows us. He knows about the sparrow and each hair of our heads. He has a purpose for us."

I studied him.

"Do you really believe that?" I asked.

"Yes, I do!" he answered with conviction.

"Then why doesn't He do something, instead of sitting quiescently on a great big white throne in the no-place called heaven?"

Dusty considered for a moment. Then he said,

"Maybe He does . . . maybe He does . . . but we cannot see everything He is doing now. Maybe our vision isn't very good at this point, 'for here we see as in a glass darkly.' But we shall see and understand sometime. We have to go on living and hoping, having faith that life is stronger than death. Only God can give life. We have to receive it—and that daily."

He hesitated, searching his memory for some thought that eluded him. Then he brightened and said,

"Here's a verse I've always found to be of help. It makes us realize that God is closer than we think:

> 'No one could tell me where my soul might be
> I sought for God, but God eluded me
> I sought my brother out and found all three
> My soul, my God, and all humanity.'

"That's about all that I can say," he concluded.

As Dusty was picking up his things, Dinty Moore came in. I remarked to him,

"Dusty and I have been having a little argument. He was telling me that God has a purpose for all of us and that we can learn something about that purpose by loving God and man. Is that right, Dusty?"

"That's right." Dusty smiled pleasantly. My attack on his beliefs had not upset him. Dinty now contributed his own piece of wisdom.

"Remember that old saying at home? 'We are a' Jock Tamson's bairns and we've a' got to hang together.'"

"And what's it supposed to mean?" I asked.

Dinty laughed, cocked his head, and screwed up his face as if asking himself the question.

"Well, you might say it means—wait a minute—hmm—you might say it means—that we are all God's children and we've all got to stick together. How's that?"

"It's pretty good, I should think."

Dusty nodded his agreement.

"Rabbie Burns must have had that at the back of his mind," Dinty went on, "when he wrote, 'For a' that, and a' that, It's comin' yet for a' that, That man to man, the world o'er, shall brothers be for a' that.'"

"I remember it well," said Dusty. "Dad was forever quoting it."

He bade us good-night; Dinty set about making me comfortable.

Next day when Dusty returned he said jubilantly,

"I've found it!"

"Found what?" I asked.

"I've found the passage I was looking for—the one that sums up what we were talking about last night. Here—I'll read it to you."

He opened his Bible to the New Testament and read aloud from the letter of St. John:

"There is no fear in love; but perfect love casteth out fear; because fear hath torment. He that feareth is not made perfect in love. We love him, because he first loved us. If a man say, I love God, and hateth his brother, he is a liar: for he that loveth not his brother whom he hath seen, how can he love God whom he hath not seen? And this commandment have we from him, That he who loveth God love his brother also."

I lay back on my sleeping platform and let myself dwell on those words. There was truth in them. Both Dusty and Dinty exemplified them.

For the first time I understood. Dusty was a Methodist—Dinty a Roman Catholic. Yet in each it was their faith that lent a special grace to their personalities; through them faith expressed a power, a presence, greater than themselves.

I was beginning to see that life was infinitely more complex, and at the same time more wonderful, than I had ever imagined. True, there was hatred. But there was also love. There was death, but there was also life. God had not left us. He was with us, calling us to live the divine life in fellowship.

I was beginning to feel the miracle that God was working in the Death Camp by the River Kwai.

CHAPTER 6

"For Thou Art with Me"

THANKS TO THE FAITHFUL CARE OF DUSTY AND Dinty, I was now on my way to recovery. True, I still suffered from malaria and dysentery, and my legs were weak and shaky, but I could get around with the aid of my staff. Compared to my condition in the Death House, I was the picture of health.

With my physical strength returning and with time to think things over, I decided I was too much of a spectator. I was allowing others to minister to me.

I asked myself the question: Why was I on the fence? Perhaps it was because of my disappointment in being captured almost at the end of a well-planned attempt to escape. Perhaps it was my resentment at wasting the good years of my youth in prison camp when I might have been playing an active part in the world struggle. Perhaps these and other things had made me bitter.

But the examples of Dusty and Dinty and the self-sacrificing heroism of Angus, the Argyll, and the Aussie were making me humble.

In this mood I saw I had to take my place with whatever was good, and begin to give what I had to offer, however small it might be. Around me men were overcoming diseases and recovering their spirits.

Although not entirely conscious of it at the time, I was

114

responding to the power of life and renewal in our midst. This was indeed a miracle, for we were without medicines; we were devoid of the props of society that make for hope.

Were others feeling as I was? I wondered. Were they, too, becoming aware that there is more to life than bread and bacon, pounds and dollars, Cadillacs and Rolls-Royces?

Were we all coming out of the figurative Death House that our lives had become—out of the spiritual pit where fear, selfishness, hatred, and despair are dominant?

Then Reason reasserted its voice. The facts hardly warranted such an assumption. There was still nearly as much sickness as ever. Men were still dying daily.

"Aren't you allowing your imagination to get the better of you?" Reason whispered. "Isn't part of the cure the wish to be cured? Aren't you allowing your latent optimism to run wild?"

"Maybe so," I had to admit. "Maybe it's only that I'm getting used to my diseases and the environment, that I am making my adjustment to these unfamiliar patterns of existence. Or it may be simply that my glands are functioning a bit better."

Then I heard the other voice:

"Perhaps all this is true. But there may be more to it than that. There may *be* a power beyond that of nature and of men. Haven't you seen it for yourself at work in Dusty and Dinty? Haven't you heard the evidence in the sacrifices of others? Possibly there is another form of healing—one that comes from the Most High."

One evening an Australian sergeant whom I had never met before came to see me. We squatted on the ground in front of my shack and talked of this and that. He had something on his mind, but it took him a little time before he could bring himself to speak of it. Finally he said,

"My cobbers and I have been talking things over. We got

to wondering if maybe there isn't something in this Christianity business after all—something we haven't understood aright in the past."

"How did that happen?" I asked.

The sergeant frowned.

"We're fed up with all we see around here," he went on. "Men kicking their mates in the teeth when they're down— stealing from each other and from the dead ones—crawling to the Japs like rats for scraps from their swill pails . . ." His voice shook with emotion. "No sir, it ain't good, any way you look at it. It's rotten, rotten, rotten."

With some effort he regained his composure.

"Yes sir, my cobbers and I have given this a lot of thought. We've all seen the worst there is—right? Now we feel there must be something better—somewhere. So we want to have another go at this Christianity—to find out if it's absolute 'dingo' or not."

"And what if you find out that it isn't?"

The sergeant scratched his chin thoughtfully.

"Then we'll bloomin' well know that it ain't. That could be important, too."

"What's this have to do with me?" I asked.

The sergeant looked at me intently.

"My cobbers they—well, they asked me to ask you if you'd be willing to meet with them—and well, sort of lead the discussion."

"But why me? Surely there must be others who could do the job much better than I."

"They think you're right for it," he replied with slow stubbornness. "For one thing, they know you're a fighting soldier. For another, they hear you've been to university, so you ought to know something about Christianity."

I was floored by his request. I wanted to refuse immediately. But the more we talked the more I felt drawn to this man.

We were able to communicate with each other effortlessly. Was it perhaps because he had had an experience similar to my own?

To gain time while I made up my mind I queried him about his own background. He told me he had spent his boyhood in the copper mines of New South Wales where he grew used to hardship and danger. He had had little formal schooling but was endowed by nature both with intelligence and inner strength of spirit.

I had not yet given him my answer when he happened to mention that because of his interest in athletics he was organizing and training a massage team to help restore life to the legs of the paralyzed. Since he was devoting himself to others, I thought, did I have any right to refuse his request? Moreover, the concern of the cobbers must be deep or they would not have sent him to me.

"And if I do come," I parried, "do you think I'll be able to do any good?"

"Oh, I haven't a doubt of it," he replied quickly. "But I must say one word. The lads won't stand for any Sunday-School stuff. What they want is the real 'dingo.' "

"All right," I said, smiling, "I'll try to give them the real 'dingo.' But mark you, I won't promise that anything I can say will have any meaning for them."

"Oh, thank you!" He got up from the ground and held out his hand.

"Where would you like to meet?" I asked.

He thought a minute.

"You know that clump of bamboos out beyond the hospital?"

"I think so, yes."

"It's right above the latrines. We'd have some privacy there."

"Isn't that down by the Death House?"

"Yes, why?"

I laughed.

"It's all part of my past. When do we meet?"

"Would tomorrow evening be too soon?"

"Not at all. I'll be there."

He bade me good-night.

I took stock of my assets. One thing I knew for certain: in a situation as real as a prison camp there was no use discussing abstract philosophical concepts. Yet I could find little in my prewar experience that promised to be meaningful.

I'd had the usual youthful idealistic enthusiasms. David Livingstone had been one of my childhood heroes. Albert Schweitzer's life and work had been an inspiration to me. At one time I had considered becoming a foreign missionary, but gradually turned my back on such a direction, and, in doing so, turned my back on Christianity as well. Its doctrines and practices seemed irrelevant and other-worldly compared to those of my rationalist friends.

The two expressions of Christian doctrine I had encountered left me unimpressed. The first maintained that the Bible had been literally inspired, had been dictated word for word and handed to man on a silver platter. The Christian life was delineated as one of obedience to a set of arbitrary laws which seemed to me negative, restrictive, and frustrating. They required one to abjure the world and its sins, to spend time in lengthy verbal prayer, to commit oneself to a Bible study of a very literal kind, and to look upon every disaster as the consequence of sin. The chief theological emphasis was placed upon the death of Jesus Christ as a sacrifice made to appease a wrathful God.

What I found particularly hard to accept was the attitude of such Christians toward others outside their sectarian group. With the vehemence of basic uncertainty they looked upon

SETIA BERGANTI. (7-3-42 & 4-4-42)

The *Setia Berganti* was a Malay prahu. She had a long deckhouse canted like the roof of a hut. "Puts you in mind of Noah's Ark, doesn't it?" said the skipper, who drew the sketch above. She was not much to look at but she was our Argus of fortune. In her we hoped to make our escape from Sumatra to Ceylon.

Islands which we didn't know were on the map, since we had no chart, appeared off our starboard bow. We put in at one of them, called Pini.

A Japanese officer in a white uniform bellowed at us through a megaphone to draw alongside the tanker. My sketch shows us looking up at a row of hostile silent faces glaring down over the rail. We clambered up the steep rope ladder while the prahu, with sails set, edged away by herself toward the horizon.

Charles Thrale

Changi, our first prison camp, was in the former British barracks on northeast Singapore Island. Buildings for a thousand men still stood, but 40,000 were crowded into the area. P.O.W. artist Charles Thrale here shows the intense overcrowding enforced by the Japanese after prisoners refused to sign a no-escape pledge.

The clinic for emergency treatment was set up in an open tent on the parade ground at Changi. The photograph above was made from a film buried for years at the camp and dug up after the war.

At Changi we had our first contact with Japanese guards. The typical one (right) was sketched by artist Ronald Searle, a P.O.W. at Changi and other camps. Knowing they would never be held responsible for their acts of brutality, the guards wreaked their wrath on the prisoners in the form of curses, blows, and ingenious methods of torture.

Ronald Searle

Diseases of malnutrition—beriberi, pellagra, and jungle ulcers—made their first appearance at Changi. The prisoner above is suffering from beriberi.

Listlessness and despair followed quickly as men fell ill. Artist Searle has caught the bleak mood in his drawings. Many turned to prayer as a magic formula to bring release from suffering; when their prayers were not answered they fell into even blacker despair.

Charles Thrale

Packed like cattle into steaming, steel-sided, windowless boxcars, we were shipped off on a four-day trip upcountry from Changi. We did not know our destination. There was barely room in the cars for a few men to sit down; the rest of us stood. At intervals we were let out to relieve ourselves.

Carrying our packs and our tools, we marched the last lap to the new camp through endless paddy fields until we reached the site where we later built the bridge over the River Kwai. There we were loaded on barges and towed to Chungkai. Some faltered and were rounded up by shouting, cursing guards.

A collection of huts at the east end of Chungkai. At the peak there were about 40 huts made of bamboo and atap palm, each one housing some 200 men.

Guardhouses and lookout posts like this one along the perimeter of the camp were not built at Chungkai until the end neared. While I was there only a double fence, 12 feet high and made of split bamboo, surrounded the camp. But the thick hostile jungle on every side was confinement enough.

Driven beyond endurance, tormented by heat, thirst, and insects, we began to build the Railroad of Death. We worked barefoot, half-naked, never fast enough to suit our captors, while the cry of "Speedo! Speedo!" rang in our ears hour after hour. Some prisoners, unable to bear the ordeal any longer, fell down where they were and died.

Leo Rawlings

Starved and exhausted prisoners were often forced to line up in pouring rain and pitch darkness to start as much as 18 hours of work on the railroad or the bridge.

West of Chungkai the route for the Railroad of Death had to be cut through rocky hills. There the number of accidents increased. The white of the limestone was often spattered red with the blood of prisoners.

Stanley Gimson

Leo Rawlings

The bridge over the River Kwai was finished in less than two months, the Railroad of Death in twelve. We shouldered the heavy beams in the swift current, always in danger of being swept downstream. Then we manned the pile drivers and with our failing strength drove the uprights into place.

Charles Thrale

Doctors did a yeoman job in caring for the sick with no equipment at their dis-
posal. They made their own instruments for special operations out of sharpene
kitchen knives; amputations often had to be performed with a carpenter's sa
and without anesthetic.

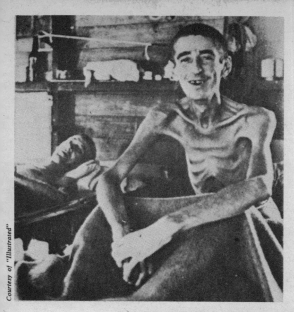

Overworked, underfed—our diet was only a handful of gummy rice a day—P.O.W.'s were soon reduced to living skeletons. In the eyes of some the spark of life still burned; in others, it had been extinguished—their spirits had been killed while they still breathed.

Stanley Gimson

The cookhouse where meals were prepared for the prisoners at Chungkai. Our rice was boiled in the open pots made of clay and iron shown in the foreground. The square cans (right) used for boiling water are four-gallon gasoline tins.

Charles Thrale

Chungkai, like every camp, had a run-down hospital hut which was known as the Death House, for few returned from it alive. The moment came when I, too, no longer able to work because my legs were paralyzed, found myself headed for the Death House.

Charles Thrale

Before the spiritual resurgence, our dead were thrown into an open pit and buried without ceremony. Exceptions were the cholera victims whose bodies were burned on a funeral pyre by the river. Here the corpses of those who had once been husbands, brothers, friends, writhed and kicked in their eerie dance of farewell as the flames leaped up.

Stanley Gimson

This is the way Chungkai looks today. After the spiritual rebirth, every man who had died was buried in a grave of his own with his name and particulars carved on a bamboo cross. The permanent cemetery was established by the War Graves Commission after the end of hostilities.

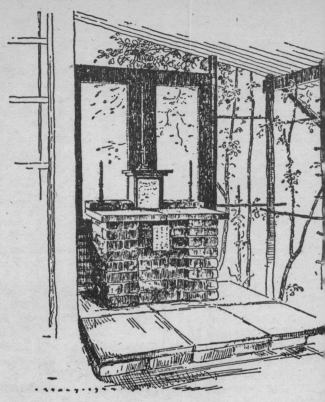

Our church of the captivity was a church without walls. No one could te[ll]
where it began or where it ended. Within it, however, prayerful hands ha[d]
fashioned a Holy Table patterned after the one above, built at Changi. O[n]
it were placed a vessel made from a tin can with a shoelace for a wick, a[nd]
a bamboo cross. A roof of atap palm protected the Holy Table from th[e]
elements.

themselves as God's anointed and were therefore critical of everyone else.

As far as I could see, they managed to extract the bubbles from the champagne of life, leaving it flat, insipid, and tasteless. I liked the world and life. I liked good companionship and laughter. Any creed which necessitated not going to the theater, not drinking, not smoking, and not kissing the lassies seemed not only monotonously dull, but an incredibly easy way of getting to heaven. I infinitely preferred a robust hell to this gray, sunless abode of the faithful where everyone was angry with everyone else.

The other expression seemed to hold that Christianity was only for nice people who had been brought up in nice homes and gone to nice schools where they had learned to do all the nice things. Heaven for this group was a kind of continuous tea party with thin cucumber sandwiches and smoky-tasting tea served in fine bone china cups. It was all eminently respectable but rather hard on those outside the pale.

None of that appealed to me. Politics or social service— something of that sort—offered me a more realistic way to help solve the problems of mankind. Then there were the sciences. The rapid progress being made in that sphere indicated that man could take care of himself and unravel his own dilemma without help from a divine power, no matter how benign.

Many brave new worlds were built in those days, and mine was one of them. We had no idea how soon they would crumble.

As I made my evaluation I decided that about my only advantage was starting with a clean slate. The next obvious thing was to find out as much as I could about Jesus.

Once, as a student, I had gone to a lecture advertised as the first in a series dealing with the person and teaching of Jesus. The series began with the Book of Leviticus in the Old

Testament. It was not clear to me how anyone could learn much about Jesus from the variety of sacrifices reported there in abundance, so I never went to another lecture. From experiences such as these I had reached the conclusion that Jesus was a figure in a fairy story, suitable for children, perhaps, but not for men.

The logical place for me to begin now, I reflected, was with the New Testament, as the only record of his life and teaching available.

I had a Bible. It was an old one which had been given to me by a kindly "other rank," who wished to lighten his pack as he set out for a trip farther upcountry. It was well-thumbed, torn, and patched, and covered with the oilskin of a gas cape. There were no references, explanations, or annotations.

That Bible was all I had to draw on when I faced the group next evening in the bamboo grove. I was not a little dismayed to see that there were several dozen of them.

They were waiting for me in respectful silence. But their faces held a look of warning which plainly said, "We'll tolerate you, chum, so long as you don't try any waffling." (Waffling is the gentle art of evading the issue or of making a half-lie take the place of the whole truth.)

I began by describing my own uncertain state of grace, telling them frankly of my doubts and conflicts. When I asked them straight out if they were willing to go along with me and face up to the basic issues of human existence, they said that they were.

At first I felt my way cautiously. I told them something of what I had learned in school of Greek and Roman culture, of polytheism and Mithraism, of the life and times of the Old Testament. It did not take me long to run through my superficial erudition. Silence fell; an uncomfortable silence. In desperation I asked for questions.

It was a risky thing to do. They might have ruined me by

driving me into a corner or forcing me into a contest of words in which I'd be the loser. But that wasn't why they were here. They wanted to find meaning in life, if meaning there was to be found.

They were very kind, those cobbers. When they began to talk they spoke freely of their own inner questioning. They gave their honest views about life on earth, its object and the life hereafter. They were seeking a truth they would be able to apprehend with the heart as well as the mind. When the meeting ended, I knew I could go on.

At each successive gathering the numbers grew. There were new faces, more and more pairs of eyes to look questioningly into mine. I expounded the New Testament in their language, keeping one lesson ahead of them.

Through our readings and our discussions we came to know Jesus. He was one of us. He would understand our problems because they were the sort of problems he had faced himself. Like us, he often had no place to lay his head, no food for his belly, no friends in high places.

He, too, had known bone-weariness from too much toil, the suffering, rejection and disappointments that are part of the fabric of life. Yet he was no killjoy. He would not have scorned the man who took a glass of wine with his friends or a mug of MacEwan's ale, or who smiled approvingly at a pretty girl. The friends he had were like our own and like us.

As we read and talked, he became flesh and blood. We saw him in the full dignity of manhood. He was a man we could understand and admire; the kind of friend we would like to have guarding our left flank; a leader we could follow.

We were fascinated by his humanity. Here was a working man, yet one who was perfectly free, who had not been enslaved by society, economics, law, politics, or religion. Demonic forces had existed then as now. They had sought to destroy him but they had not succeeded.

True, he had been strung up on a cross and tormented with the hell of pain; but he had not broken. The weight of law and of prejudice had borne down on him but failed to crush him. He had remained free and alive, as the resurrection affirmed. What he was, what he did, what he said, all made sense for us. We understood that the love expressed so supremely in Jesus was God's love—the same love we were experiencing for ourselves—the love that is passionate kindness, other-centered rather than self-centered, greater than all the laws of men. It was the love that inspired St. Paul, once he had felt its power, to write:

"Love suffereth long and is kind."

The doctrines we worked out were meaningful to us. We approached God through Jesus the carpenter of Nazareth, the incarnate word. Such an approach seemed logical, for that was the way he had come to us. He had taken flesh, walked in the midst of men, and declared himself by his actions to be full of grace and truth.

We arrived at our understanding of God's ways not one by one, but together. In the fellowship of freedom and love we found truth, and with truth a wonderful sense of unity, of harmony, of peace.

While we were conducting our nightly sessions in the bamboo grove, as soon as I was able I joined the Australian sergeant's massage team. Each of us was assigned four or five patients to care for, scattered in different huts throughout the camp. We visited our charges daily. As we massaged we listened to their woes and worries. When the opportunity came we talked, seeking to impart assurance, encouraging their will to live.

Nearly all of our patients were young. Some of them were dying. I had reason then to be thankful for the eternal truths that we had found during our meetings in the bamboo grove. Almost daily, questions were asked of me for which reason had no answer. Almost daily, I was brought face to face with the great problems of human experience.

These queries took many forms. But nearly all of them were only concealments for the Big One: "How do I face death? Can death be overcome?"

Reason had no more to say on this subject than "there's nothing to life beyond the fact that we are born, we suffer, and we die." Most of us were accustomed to such an answer, for it had been stamped indelibly on our subconscious minds by the many conditioning processes of the twentieth century. This may have sufficed for normal living, but for men dying away from home in a jungle prison camp, it was not enough.

When an acceptable answer was demanded of me, I had to go beyond Reason—I had to go to Faith. If I had learned to trust Jesus at all, I had to trust him here. Reason said, "We live to die." Jesus said, "I am the resurrection and the life."

In the light of our new understanding, the Crucifixion was seen as being of the utmost relevance to our situation. A God who remained indifferent to the plight of His creatures was not a God with whom we could agree. The Crucifixion, however, told us that God was in our midst, suffering with us.

We did not know the complete answer to the problem of suffering, but we could see that so much of it was caused by "man's inhumanity to man," by selfishness, by greed, and by all the forces of death that we readily support in the normal course of life. The cry of the innocent child, the agony I had seen in the eyes of a Chinese mother as she carried her dead baby, the suffering caused by earthquakes, fire, or floods, we could not explain. But we could see that God was not indifferent to such suffering.

We stopped complaining about our own. Faith would not

save us from it, but it would take us through it. Suffering no longer locked us up in the prison house of self-pity but brought us into what Albert Schweitzer calls the "fellowship of those who bear the mark of pain." We looked at the Cross and took strength from the knowledge that it gave us, the knowledge that God was in our midst.

Our lives were never free from the shadow of sadness. Our faith was tested daily by the suffering which we saw all around us, which we were now trying with our limited means and new-found truths to assuage.

I was walking back to my hut one evening when a medical orderly from the hospital stopped me.

"Excuse me, sir," he said. "There's an Argyll in my ward who'd like to see you. He came in a couple days ago with a sick party from upcountry. He's a young lad."

"How did he know I was here?"

"I found out he was an Argyll when I was making a note of his particulars. I remarked about your trying to help the boys by giving massage."

"Does he need massage?"

"No. There's nothing we can do. He's dying. He has gangrene. It's all through him."

"What would you like me to do, then?"

"He's so miserable, I thought perhaps you could comfort him. In any case, he'll be glad to see another Argyll."

"Take me to him," I said.

The long hut to which the orderly led me was crowded with new arrivals. We made our way down the row of sleeping platforms astir with the restless movements of men in pain.

Near the center of the hut he stopped beside a motionless figure. The orderly must have been accustomed to seeing youngsters die. But something about this one seemed to have touched him. The dim light accentuated both the boy's youth and his loneliness.

"Here he is, lad," the orderly said softly. "I've brought him to you."

Large, frightened gray eyes stared up at me from an emaciated face. I bent closer. He seemed to recognize me.

"Oh, I'm so glad to see you, sir."

He managed to sit up.

"I'm glad to see *you*," I replied.

"Perhaps you don't know me," he said. "I arrived with the last draft. I've seen you often, but you probably haven't seen me."

The last draft I remembered only too well. Those who had been sent to us were boys of eighteen. With but half a year's training, and school or apprenticeship only months behind them, they had been plunged into the bloodiest of actions, and the survivors into the worst kind of imprisonment.

He began to speak rapidly as though a great weight had been lifted from him.

"I've been so lonely. I don't know anyone here. It's been a long time since I've seen an Argyll."

"You're looking at one now," I said, smiling. "And there are others. You'll find friends here."

I sat down on the narrow edge of his sleeping platform.

"It's been hard for you, hasn't it?"

"Awfully hard," he nodded without self-consciousness. "I've become terribly depressed. I suppose because I'm scared. I'm so scared at times I can't think."

"What are you scared of?"

"Oh—scared about the Nips—and scared that I'm going to die."

What could I say? I knew he didn't have a chance because of the advanced state of his gangrene. I looked at him, lying there so lonely and so young, and said the only thing I could think of,

"We'll help you not to be scared. We'll stay by you."

That seemed to ease his mind.

"Thank you, sir," he said. "That's good to know."

He gave me an engaging boyish grin. I got up.

"Go to sleep now. I'll look in on you tomorrow."

I did what I could for him, but it hurt because it was so little. I passed the word to Dusty and Dinty. They went to see him often, and, in turn, encouraged their friends to do so. Soon the lad had a chain of regular visitors; he did not spend too many hours alone.

I had been able to obtain some delicacies for him—a duck egg and half a hand of bananas. I went to take these to him.

"How are things tonight?" I asked.

I was delighted at the change in his manner. He seemed relaxed and almost cheerful.

"Not too bad," he said, sitting up. "You've no idea what a help it is to have friends. I don't feel lonely any more. And I'm not scared."

He smiled up at me trustingly. Then, very softly, he said, "I'm going to die, am I not?"

I cleared my throat, searching for words.

"That's a possibility we all have to face. I've faced it—so have a lot of others."

"I know." The boy nodded. "That's why I like to talk to you. You've been through it. You understand."

I did not answer. I was thinking to myself,

"Do I? Do I? Can I ever understand even a little of what goes on in another's mind and heart?"

His tremulous smile was fading. A frown of worry wrinkled his forehead as he looked at me.

"My mother and dad will miss me. I'm the only one they have and they'll be so lonely when I don't come back."

He gave a little sigh.

"It's hard to be young and to have to die. I don't even know what this war is all about."

"Here, let me read you something that may help." I spoke the words evenly, pretending to be more in control of my emotions than I actually was.

I had brought my Bible with me. I opened its torn pages and in the dim light of the hut I began to read those words that had brought solace to countless souls before him,

" 'Yea, though I walk through the valley of the shadow of death, I will fear no evil: for thou art with me; thy rod and thy staff they comfort me.' "

I looked at him. He was lying quietly. I turned to another passage.

" 'I am the resurrection and the life; he that believeth in me, though he were dead, yet shall he live: And whosoever liveth and believeth in me shall never die. Believest thou this?' "

I put the Bible down. His gray eyes were far away. He was listening within himself—to the message these words had brought. After a bit he turned his gaze to mine and said with perfect calm,

"Everything is going to be all right."

"Yes," I said, nodding, "everything is going to be all right."

He slumped back. His efforts had exhausted him. I knelt beside his sleeping platform and gently stroked his forehead with my fingers until he fell into a deep, untroubled sleep.

Two evenings later, on my way to visit him again, I saw the orderly coming toward me on the run.

"Quickly!" he cried. "He hasn't long to go."

Together we ran. The boy was lying there without moving.

"Hello, son," I said. At the sound of my voice he turned his face toward me.

"Hello, sir. I'm glad you're here."

I knelt beside him and took his pathetically thin hand in

mine. A yellow glow lighted up the darkness behind me. The thoughtful orderly had produced a coconut-oil lamp.

"Light," said the boy in his low voice. "It's good to have light. I don't like the dark."

The flame rose and fell then burned steadily, holding back the shadows.

"It's all right. I'm glad it's all right," he whispered. There was a look of trust and hope on his face as he said this.

"Yes, my son, it's all right," I assured him. "God our Father is with us. He is very near." My voice was husky.

"I know He is." The sigh the boy gave was not sad, but confident.

Still holding his hand, I prayed,

" 'Our Father which art in heaven, Hallowed be thy name. . . .' "

His eyes were closed. But as I watched his face I could see his lips repeating the words with me.

" '. . . Thy kingdom come. . . .' "

The lamp grew dim, then burned more brightly.

" '. . . Thy will be done in earth as it is in heaven. . . .' "

His lips no longer moved. His breath started coming in great sobbing gasps. They ceased. He was quiet—with the quietness of death.

"Father," I prayed, "receive this dear child. Welcome him with Thy love for the sake of Jesus Christ, our Savior, Thy Son. Amen."

I put down his hand by his side, smoothed his hair, and wiped my tears from his forehead.

His was not an isolated case. The awareness of the tragedy of dying young was keenly felt by so many lads who faltered on the threshold of death.

A fragment of some poetry, written in Singapore by one of them, an unknown English youth, came into my possession. His lines express the feeling of many:

"What shall I think when I am called to die?
Shall I not find too soon my life has ended?
The years, too quickly, have hastened by
With so little done of all that I'd intended.

"There were so many things I'd meant to try
So many contests I had hoped to win
And lo, the end approaches just as I
Was thinking of preparing to begin."

It was experiences such as these that made our discussions in the bamboo grove meaningful. We were developing a keener insight into life and its complexities. We were learning what it means to be alive—to be human. As we became more aware of our responsibility to God the Father, we realized that we were put in this world not to be served but to serve. This truth touched and influenced many of us to some degree, even those who shunned any religious quest. There was a general re-awakening. Men began to smile—even to laugh—and to sing.

I was hobbling back to my shack after a rather late discussion session. Passing one of the huts, I stopped. I thought I heard the sound of men singing. They were singing—singing "Jerusalem the Golden." Someone was beating time on a piece of tin with a stick.

The words of the grand old hymn seemed symbolic to me as I listened. Maybe Jerusalem, the Kingdom of God, is here after all, "with milk and honey blest." Maybe man "shall not live by bread alone" (or "rice alone," as we were literally doing). Maybe there is the milk and honey of the spirit that puts hope into a man's eyes and a song on his lips.

They went on as I stood there, singing the hymn once more. The song made the darkness seem friendly. In the difference between this joyful sound and the joyless stillness of months past was the difference between life and death.

This hymn had the sound of victory. To me it said,

"Man need never be so defeated that he can do nothing. Weak, sick, broken in body, far from home, and alone in a strange land, he can sing! He can worship!"

The resurgence of life increased. It grew and leavened the whole camp, expressing itself in men's concern for their neighbors.

There were many instances of this.

The most forlorn, the most dispirited among the bedridden, were the amputees. The loss of legs was common among us —the end result of tropical ulcers and the many diseases stemming from malnutrition. Amputation—performed with a carpenter's saw and without benefit of anesthetic—was often a last resort to stop gangrene and save lives.

We were taking preventive measures now through our work on the massage teams. But those who were beyond this type of help could only lie or sit on their sleeping platforms, unable to move about.

In one of the huts a friendship developed between a cobbler and an engineer. The engineer had an inventive mind; the cobbler was adept with his hands. They took long walks together, animatedly discussing some project. Presently they were seen working with odd scraps of material.

One day they gathered their hutmates and disclosed what they had been doing. They had produced an artificial leg. It was a workmanlike article: the foot was a block of wood secured to a bamboo leg by strips of tin from old cans and by pieces of leather. The leg supported a round basket of leather and canvas to hold the stump. It even boasted an ingenious tin joint which enabled the wearer to bend his knee when he sat down or to lock it into rigidity when he wished to walk.

The other P.O.W.'s examined it with admiring curiosity.

Quite a thing. Good job they'd made of it. But of what practical value was one leg where hundreds were needed?

The cobbler and the engineer then offered their proposal: They would teach the amputees to make other legs just like it. With Mark One off the drawing board, it shouldn't prove too difficult to go into mass production. It was a matter only of finding the raw materials.

Thus was born in Chungkai a new industry—run by the legless—for the legless.

Volunteers caught the spirit and went out scrounging for any odds and ends that could be useful. Some brought hides from the slaughterhouse, others, sections of bamboo or knapsacks to be cut up into canvas strips. Some slipped out beyond the fence at night to bring back pods of yellow silky kapok that grew wild in the jungle, for kapok was ideally suited to line the stump-supporting baskets.

When the amputees had mastered their new trade, they expanded their production and also made sandals for their mates who still had legs. These sandals were far from a perfect fit—but they fulfilled their purpose of covering a man's foot, and of protecting it against cuts and bruises.

With mobility, and work to fill the idle hours came new hope —not only for those who were able to move around the camp for the first time, but for the many others who had been haunted by the fear that they too might lose their legs.

The new legs functioned; the new industry flourished.

While I was passing the work area one evening I heard a *click-clack-thud-thud; click-clack-thud-thud*. I saw a cocky little man strutting proudly along on two artificial legs.

"That's quite a performance you're giving," I said admiringly.

He winked at me.

"You haven't seen nothing yet," he replied happily. "Keep your eye on me. When I get these pistons working properly I'll

be the fastest man in camp. The hundred yards in ten seconds
—that's what I'll be doing."

Click-clack-thud-thud; click-clack-thud-thud—it made a
lively sound as he went off into the dusk.

Along with our awakening came a spontaneous hunger for
education. Exhausted as men were by their work on the railroad, and subjected as they were daily to cruelties and depriva-
tions in the camp, their minds were very much alive. To satisfy
this hunger, a jungle university was established. Perhaps
"established" is too grand a word, for it was a university without lecture halls, without trustees or an admissions office, without a campus. Classes were held anywhere, at any time.

Inquiring students sought out their masters among those
who'd had the benefit of special training and practically shang-
haied them into serving as *magistri*. A group would gather
around a teacher in a given discipline and there we'd have a
seminar. As rapidly as students learned, they would put their
knowledge at the service of their fellow P.O.W.'s by acting as
the leaders of other seminars. The taught became the teachers
in a chain reaction. The only qualification for admission to any
class was a thirst for knowledge.

The curriculum, for those circumstances, was amazingly
varied. Courses were offered in history, philosophy, economics, mathematics, several of the sciences, and at least nine
languages. The languages included Latin, Greek, Russian, and
Sanskrit.

The instructors were not deterred by the shortage of textbooks. They wrote their own, from memory, as they went
along. Language teachers compiled their own grammars on
odd scraps of paper.

A library was formed. It was a peripatetic library. It had
no home, no lending system. Men made known the books
they had and arranged by word of mouth to pass them on to
others.

As the library grew the presence in camp of a surprising variety of books was brought to light. The library of Raffles College in Singapore had been plundered by the Japanese, and a number of volumes found their way to Changi, and thence to Chungkai.

Men had clung to any books that fell into their hands—for practical reasons. They were useful for barter. The pages were prized for rolling cigarettes, for writing letters home, or for use as toilet paper. Now the situation was reversed. Books were again valued for their contents.

By the good graces of gifted teachers I was able to resume the study of law which I had begun in the Army. In addition, I combined the study of Greek and moral philosophy by reading Plato's *Republic* and Aristotle's *Nicomachean Ethics* in the original. I obtained these books through the generosity of an Oxford classicist. They were his most precious possessions.

Before long I found myself teaching what I was learning to two groups of my own. One group wanted to study elementary Greek; the other, subjects of ethical concern.

I had no Greek grammar. By searching my own memory and by probing the memories of friends, I was able to write out an elementary working grammar on paper scraps, which was passed from student to student. The Japanese at that period were taking pleasure in subjecting us during the day to prolonged roll calls. My pupils made good use of the time by memorizing the conjugations or declensions they were in process of learning as they stood on parade.

My study group in ethics was no doubt typical of many gatherings. It was comprised of three Australians, two Englishmen, and three Scots. All were as different as could be in background and in education. One had been a professional boxer, one a rancher, one a university student, one a laboratory technician, one a carpenter, one a high school student, one an insurance clerk, and one a teacher. But all had in common both intellectual curiosity and enthusiasm.

We met about three times a week either at the side of one of the huts or by one of the few bamboo clumps still left in the ever-expanding camp.

Beginning with the *Republic* we discussed successive theories that have patterned the minds of people in different societies. One in particular that provoked vehement argument was the theory of utilitarianism.

"Blimey," said one of the Diggers, sitting cross-legged on the ground, "if efficiency is the test of goodness then we'll end up by being part of a ruddy great machine. It's only machines that work efficiently."

An Englishman said authoritatively,

"But if the state has to assure the greatest happiness of the greatest number then it has to be governed and administered with the maximum of efficiency."

"Oh, to hell with that!" the Digger retorted impatiently. "That kind of efficiency means the guys at the top telling the rest of us wot we must do. Take our proper place in society and all that rot. No, I'm not for it. Wot's goin' to happen to the poor blokes who ain't in the greatest number? Tell me that!"

"They'll be educated, I suppose," the Englishman said coolly, "until they learn to respect the best interests of others."

"Browbeaten, that's what they'll be!" said the Digger. "The sods who write the textbooks will try to control our minds."

"What would you expect in an 'ideal' society?" I asked.

"Me freedom," the Digger shot back at me. "Me freedom to think me own thoughts and to live me own life the way I bloomin' well fancy."

"That would lead to anarchy," said the Englishman quietly.

"And wot's wrong with a healthy bit of anarchy, I'd like to know? I'm going to use some of it when I get back to tell old Menzies wot I think of him for gettin' us into this mess.''

"If everybody did that sort of thing, where do you think it would get us?" inquired the Englishman.

"It might get us some peace, that's wot!" came the Australian's voice from the darkness. "Trouble is, a bloke never has the chance to say what he wants. If all the blokes in the world were to tell the bosses in government that we weren't going to fight no more ruddy wars for them, then we could stay at home and take the old girl out swimming at Bondi Beach."

There was general laughter and a murmuring of approval.

"That's what the League of Nations tried to do, wasn't it?" called out a Scottish voice with a Glasgow accent.

"No, it bloody well didn't, mate," retorted the Australian promptly. "Damn few of the blokes in the world ever knew there was such a thing as the League of Nations. It was for all them smooth-tongued bastards in spats and monkey suits— that's what it was for."

"Those chaps in spats," said the quiet English voice, "are our duly elected representatives."

"Not mine, they ain't!"

I asked the Australian,

"How would you run things? Let's hear what you've got in mind."

"By not runnin' them," he replied quickly. "There's too many blockheads runnin' things as it is. The way things are, the state controls us by force and says it does it for our own good. The difference between a tyranny and a democracy, as I see it, is one of degree—the degree of force that is used."

"But we've got to have force to preserve law and order," a new voice broke in.

"No we ain't!" said the Australian hotly. "We don't have to live by force, see! We only think we do."

"What do you mean, 'think we do'?" someone jeered.

"Cor, we've been told that, ain't we? That's why we studied history at school. History was just one bloody war after another to prove that the simple blokes of the earth have to be kept under control by force."

Explosive mutters of protest interrupted him.

"Now shut up and let me speak me piece," he said in a loud voice, and then continued quickly,

"Wot we blokes have to do when we get back, see, is to say, 'We've had it.' No more bleedin' force. We ain't interested in keeping on with the old ways. Wot we want is for blokes to respect each other and work with each other."

"And how the hell do you think you're going to do that?" an irritated Scottish voice called out.

"By doing it—just by doing it. We talk too much."

A sharp burst of laughter greeted this remark.

"All right—I'll give you that," said the Digger, unperturbed. "Me too. I talk too much. All of us talk too much. We do too little. We talk about democracy, freedom, brotherhood, equality, and all those words, but we don't do them, see?"

I had to interrupt.

"Wind it up, Digger. 'Lights out' is almost due."

"Okay. Well, what I've been tryin' to say is that it ain't the state we want to support, but a community."

"What you want is communism!" a voice called out.

"No, it bloody well ain't," said the Australian indignantly. "Communism just means being forced to do what the state wants and calling it equality. That's all that is . . . Let me finish! A community is people doing instead of yapping. It ain't saying we are equal—it's doing it so that it's real. It ain't shouting about truth—it's doing it. It ain't barking about peace—it's being peaceful. You get my drift?

"Look at this here camp," he continued. "A regular police state it is—run by force. Cobbers like ourselves have been trying to follow the Nips' bad example. That's why we've been tearing at each other's throats. If you ask me, we might get somewhere if we had a little respect for each other and learned to share what we have."

"All impossible—totally impossible," said the English voice conclusively.

"Like hell it is. It's only impossible because you want it to be impossible. When a gang of blokes stand up and show what they mean by what they do—then you'll see changes being made."

The call of the bugle cut him short.

"You'll see the blokes executed," said the Englishman.

We broke up. As we walked away from the bamboo grove, the Australian's final words echoed in my ears:

"—then you'll see changes being made."

"Yes," I thought to myself, "we'll see changes being made. And when we see them we'll see the Kingdom of God."

Arguments like these did not take place in a vacuum. When we returned to our huts we were confronted by an environment that was all too present and painful.

No records were kept in our university; no grades handed out; no degrees were awarded. Our courses did much to relieve the awful monotony. But they did much more than that: They helped us to see that our minds could work only on what they received through education, through experience, above all through faith. It was faith, I saw, that enabled us to transcend our environment, to appropriate what was good and true in our education and tradition, and thus prepare us to make decisions on matters of ultimate consequence to us as human beings.

It was clear that the quest for meaning, the religious search, and the hunger for knowledge all go hand in hand.

One evening a prisoner named Dodger Green came to see me after roll call. He was a fair, slight, waif-and-stray type of man who had served with me in the 93rd Highlanders.

Life had not treated him kindly. He had spent his youth in an orphanage in the north of England where he sorely missed the happy rough-and-tumble of a normal home. I had always been conscious of an air of sadness about him—something which he tried to disguise by carrying a chip on his shoulder. He was always a good soldier, though—better than he knew.

Tonight he struck me as being sadder than ever.

"I've just arrived at this camp," he said. "I heard you were here so I thought I'd come over and have a chat with you as I didn't think you'd mind."

He said this very shyly, turning his face away from me and gazing down at the ground.

"Glad to see you," I said, taking his hand. "How are things with you?"

He shook his head.

"Not so good. I had a pretty rough time upcountry and had to be sent back. My prospects ain't bright."

He seemed very much down in the mouth.

"What's wrong?" I asked.

He tapped a Dutch army canteen that he wore strapped above his right groin.

"My ruddy guts have sealed up and they end with a hole in my belly."

"What's the trouble?"

"Ulcers of some kind, that's what it is. My guts cemented together. The docs tell me they've grown into each other in some queer way. I don't rightly understand how."

He looked bleak.

"The M.O. says there isn't anything more can be done for me until we get out of these goddamn awful prisons."

He was such a picture of misery that I tried to cheer him up.

"The sooner we all get out the better. It may not be too long now."

He stared down at his feet.

"Maybe it *will* be too long for me—and others like me."

"Come off it," I said. "You've been through the worst. You've got to stick it out. You've friends that will help you."

Again he shook his head, as if to imply that someone like him could never expect to have friends.

"I'm not so sure about that."

His long, hollow face with the high cheekbones made him look the last word in hopelessness.

"I'll stick by you," I said. "And so will others. We'll work something out together. Let me know if there is anything I can do."

"Thank you," he said. "I don't think there is. But it was nice of you to say that."

He raised his head, and held out his hand to bid me good-night.

Dodger was going. I had done nothing for him—nothing to ease his path. I thought fast. What was there I could do that would arouse some response?

"Have you anything to read?" I asked.

"No, I haven't read anything for a long time. I did have a detective story—but it was pinched from me—along with my mess kit."

He brightened.

"Yes, now that you speak of it, I would like to read again."

A couple of days before I'd borrowed a novel.

"I've a book I think you'll like. It's Richard Llewellyn's *How Green Was My Valley*. I've just finished it and I'll be glad to lend it to you. It's a great book."

Before giving it to him I took a few bahts—and slipped them between the pages. They were all the money I had. Then I wished him good-night.

Next day he came back to see me. Holding out the baht notes, he said gruffly,

"You left something in the book. Here it is."

He looked so self-righteous standing there that I couldn't help smiling.

"Surely you don't believe I'm so wealthy that I can afford to use money for book markers, do you? Even those that have been printed by the Japanese?"

His shoulders lost their stiffness; the strain left his face.

"No, I suppose not. Did you mean for me to have them?"

"Of course I did. Take them—and buy yourself some eggs and bananas. I suppose you know by now that there's a canteen in this camp."

Rather sheepishly he said,

"I've no money—that is, I haven't had until now." He held out the bahts again. "I can't believe you want me to have these."

"That's exactly what I want," I said firmly. "Sit down and give me your crack."

He began to talk in a friendly fashion. The more he talked the more he seemed at home in my little shack. He was sitting beside me now with his two hands around his left knee, pressing it close to his chest. After a time he said,

"You know, I haven't had much of an education, but I get to thinking about things every now and again. I've never been able to talk about them with anyone before. I'd like to. Do you mind if I come to you?"

He pressed his knee against his chest all the more tightly as he said this. It had been an effort for him to make the request. He had a wistful, yet hopeful, look.

"Certainly not," I replied, thankful to have him ask me. "I'll be delighted to discuss things with you. We'll begin with the book you're reading and go on from there."

We had many talks. First, I discussed literature in general: I spoke of authors and what they were trying to say; the symbols they used to convey meaning; and the subjective quality that made reading not only entertaining but enlightening.

We took up history and the figures who made history. Gradually we came to people and their actions. What made them the way they were? Why did they act as they did? What was unique about man? Such discussions took us naturally into the realm of religion. He borrowed my Bible. Soon Dodger was reading the New Testament with understanding and enjoyment.

All the while, Dodger was becoming more cheerful, more hopeful, more relaxed, more rested. The strained and frightened look went out of his eyes. He laughed more and took more interest in the company of others.

One day he said to me,

"I'm going to look around and see if I can give a hand anywhere. I've been helping the orderlies in the hospital. But I reckon I can do more."

Eventually Dodger found how he could be of service—in a way that was badly needed. The filthiest job in camp was to collect the used ulcer rags, scrape them clean of pus, boil them, and return them for future use. A smelly, unpleasant job it was, but Dodger volunteered for it. Regularly I would see him going from hut to hut, carrying his can of rags, and whistling as he walked.

Observing him, I concluded that he had come to terms with life. He knew he hadn't much time left. What he had to do was to live out the days that remained to him moment by moment.

Dodger turned out to have hidden assets. He had a quick eye and a sharp mind, perhaps unsuspected by himself until he put them to use in the service of his comrades. He had only to learn of a particular need and he would take on the responsibility of supplying it.

Somebody lacked a bucket with which to wash himself. Dodger appeared with one he had made from a bamboo trunk. It could be carried over a man's shoulder by a strap of reeds.

A prisoner's mess tin was missing. Dodger devised one by beating two tin cans into something approximating the desired shape. Or he would provide a container he had carved from a section of bamboo.

Someone else couldn't face the rice any more. Dodger would be seen crouched over his fire with his little homemade skillet, cooking up an omelet—out of a duck egg and some lime juice.

When grateful prisoners paid him now and then for these small services, he accepted the money without protest. Then he used it to buy food for those in need.

The last time I saw him, his slight figure was moving energetically along, intent on some errand for a comrade. He conveyed the impression of a man happy and fulfilled by having a purpose.

Our new hope and feeling for life also found expression in a burst of artistic activity. In one hut a carved head would appear, in another, a blueprint of a yacht; in another, a collection of cartoons or portraits in color.

The P.O.W.'s could hardly have turned to the arts at a less propitious time. But under the urge to give meaning to their lives, they exhibited remarkable resourcefulness.

For those who wanted to try carving, raw materials were at hand; the jungle abounded in all kinds of wood, some of it beautiful in hue and texture.

Artists made their own pigments from the most improbable materials: crushed charcoal, pulverized rock, even boiled book covers. They made brushes from human hair plucked from their own beards.

Before long, enough creations of various kinds had been accumulated so that it was decided to hold an exhibition at the end of one of the huts. The work of thirty or forty P.O.W.'s was represented.

On display were carved or sculptured heads; blueprints or pen drawings of sailing ships; portraits of hutmates, of wives or girl friends.

An exhibitor did pictures of his children as he imagined they must look now. When he left home, one had been not more than a year old; the other had just been born. He had not seen them for four years.

The first response of the visitors to the improvised gallery was one of surprise that there should be such talent among us. The next reaction was to wonder if they couldn't do just as well themselves. Thus each wave of artistic expression set off succeeding waves.

Then there was the orchestra.

I was standing outside my hut talking to another Argyll, Bill Maclean, when we saw a friend of ours, an officer in the Indian Army, heading toward us.

"Blimey!" said Bill. "What's that Jim's got in his hand? I can't believe it! That's a violin."

A shipment from the International Y.M.C.A. with an assortment of games and food parcels had reached the camp.

"Six fiddles were among the games," Jim explained. "The Japs can't eat 'em or sell 'em. So they figured if they turned the violins over to us, they could report they'd distributed the parcels. That would make it only two-thirds a lie, which is a good deal closer to the truth than they usually come."

Jim looked from Bill to me.

"Can either of you play one?"

Bill shook his head.

"How about you, Ernie?"

"I'll have a go at it."

I tucked the violin under my chin, tested the strings, and tightened the pegs. I had not played one since I was twelve years old.

I could see the room in my home in Scotland—the sunlight on the bright flowered wallpaper, the heavy old-fashioned mahogany chairs, the thick green curtains, and my mother seated at the upright walnut piano playing my accompaniment.

Taking the bow in my hand now, I tried to remember the pieces which I had once learned. I played a few bars, first from "O Sole Mio," then from "The Blue Danube Waltz."

As I scraped away I had a feeling I wasn't getting the best out of the instrument. I noticed Bill was gritting his teeth. Then Jim said,

"Coo! That's ruddy awful. The Nips'll think we're castrating a tomcat."

"You don't appreciate good classical music, that's your trouble," I retorted.

"That was neither good, nor classical, nor music," said Jim.

"But why must you find someone who can play the fiddle?" I asked. Jim went on to explain that now that the violins had come, there was a plan afoot to form an orchestra. The Japanese had given their permission, because they wanted to be entertained. "Takes more than a few fiddles to make an orchestra," I reminded him.

Bill put in,

"What are you going to do about the other instruments?"

"And not only the instruments," I said. "What about the scores and all that sort of thing? Where are they going to come from?"

"Norman has everything in hand," said Jim. "Do you know Norman?"

"Oh, yes, we know him," Bill replied. "He's a member in good standing of our club."

"Club?" Jim looked at us quizzically.

"The Amoebic Dysentery Club. It's quite democratic. The only requirement for membership is a bloody stool."

With Norman at the helm we were confident that whatever the obstacles, the camp would have an orchestra. Norman was what my cobbers called "a Dingo kid." In spite of the fact the parasites had done their worst to him, he still had remarkable enthusiasm and drive—especially where his first love, music, was concerned.

Music was the passion of his life. He wanted it to be his profession. But his family expected him to make money instead of music, so he had taken a job with a bank somewhere in the City. In his spare time he was conductor of a music society in the London neighborhood where he lived. He also played several instruments himself. Gifted with a photographic memory, he could reproduce the parts for any instruments on demand.

The brasses, Jim told us, were already pretty well organized. Norman had canvassed the camp and flushed several trumpets, trombones, and saxophones, which, surprisingly enough, prisoners had somehow managed to keep with them. The musicians for the woodwinds section were already hard at work making their own instruments. I wanted to know where on earth they obtained their materials.

"Bamboo," said Jim. "Bamboo, remember, comes in all sizes."

"But how do you go about making a woodwind out of bamboo?" Bill asked. "The whole thing sounds impossible."

"Far from it. In fact, we're already nearly up to full strength. I'm no woodwind musician myself, but I'll try to tell you how it's done. First you choose a bamboo with the right diameter and cut it to the length you want. Then you put a plug in one end, leaving room for the reed. Now comes the hard part— you start boring holes with a penknife to get the right notes. So you bore and then you test with a pitch pipe—or tuning whistle—which turned up in camp. You do this until you have just the note you want, d'you see?"

This accounted for the strange peeping noises we'd been hearing lately from some of the huts.

"It's quite simple, actually. All you need is patience."

Jim went on to tell us about some of the other instruments.

"One chap is making his own bass viol," he said. "He was able to scrounge some tea boxes. He cut the wood into strips and glued them together. Then he had to have the strings, but they were easy. He visited the Nip slaughterhouse, helped himself to the cows' guts—the Japs didn't mind because they weren't worth anything—took them home and dried them on the fence."

He waved the violin.

"And these six fiddles are a godsend to the strings section. Besides, this chap brought more guts than he can use so now we'll have spare strings for our violins. Oh, yes—and let me tell you about the percussion section—"

This, too, was assuming promising proportions. The men had made four or five kettledrums by taking old oil barrels, hammering them down to differing depths, and stretching hides from the slaughterhouse over the tops. The ends of those same barrels made satisfactory cymbals.

I asked what they proposed to do about the scores.

"They used all the paper scraps they could find," Jim said. Norman got the idea of writing instrumental parts on the white insides of large bamboo sections. They'll be a little awkward to handle, I expect, but they're better than nothing."

We tried to picture what this orchestra would look like with its odd array of instruments and the strangest kind of parts.

The monsoon season was coming on, the time of dispiriting wetness which we dreaded. But this year we were cheered up by the anticipation of our first concert. The date was set for early October.

It was an evening to remember.

To the north of the camp was an incline which made a natural amphitheater. The moment roll call was over we rushed to our outdoor concert hall, a half a mile away.

We found that our Japanese captors had already occupied the front-row seats. But no matter; there was room enough for everybody.

The prisoners quickly took their places on the ground. The sun had disappeared behind the green bamboo. Overhead the tropic blue of the sky was deepening. Darkness would soon descend.

Norman mounted the podium, and raised his baton.

I looked down over the slope. The men sat with their hands clasped around their knees, their heads nodding to the rhythm of the music. No orchestra ever could have asked for a more appreciative audience.

Norman had arranged the program wisely. He had included music for all tastes, ranging from Beethoven's *Fifth Symphony* to selections from *The Mikado*.

I looked at the listeners' faces. From their expressions I could tell that their fancies had taken wing, and were soaring far out beyond the bamboo curtain that held us in. Noble memories, long dormant, were stirred once again, helping us on our way to fulfilling the infinite possibilities of the spirit.

The night forced itself upon us, and, with the engulfing darkness, too soon, much too soon, it was over. At first there was absolute silence—the expectancy of men waiting for more, hoping for more. Then—tumultuous applause.

I glanced at my neighbor. His face was shining.

"Great! Isn't it great?" he exclaimed. The cheers and the handclapping in thunderous echo were proof that this was the unanimous opinion. Even our guards joined in.

Whenever there was a performance, no one asked, "Are you going?" Everyone was going—if he could limp or crawl or hitch along on his artificial legs—or even if he couldn't walk at all. It was by no means unusual to see a man being carried up the incline on a stretcher. In music was medicine for the soul.

One night as the orchestra was playing Schubert's *Unfinished Symphony*, I was sitting on the outside of the amphitheater, not far from the road. A sick party was being marched in from another camp. It must have been a long march, for they looked dead tired.

They were bound for the cookhouse for a bowl of rice, when the haunting strains of Schubert reached their ears. They turned their heads, they stopped, they sat down. The rice could wait.

While they listened, faces came to life. When the music had ended, I heard a little skeleton of a man near me say to his companion with feeling,

"God, that was lovely—bloody lovely!"

I thought to myself as I heard it,

"Aren't there two kinds of food—one for the body and one for the soul? And of the two, isn't the latter the more satisfying?"

The music reminded us that there is always beauty to be found in life—even amid the ashes. The party rose reluctantly, one by one, and moved on.

The orchestra remained the most important of the enhancements of life. But now others were beginning to be added.

The Japanese now granted us permission to build a stage, which made possible a variety of entertainment—from light plays and vaudeville to ballet.

A stage designer named David ffolke, who has since become well-known on both sides of the Atlantic, performed wonders in getting up the sets. He made his paints and dyes from liquid mud or boiled leaves and bark. Rice sacks and old green Japanese army mosquito nets substituted for backdrops and flats. Perhaps we thought the costumes and décor greater than they really were, for their inspired simplicity gave our imaginations much to feed on.

Fizzer Pearson, a Londoner like Norman, directed all our plays and acted in them. The plots came out of his head. Since we had no script, there was a great deal of "ad-libbing." Both the writing and the acting may have lacked polish, but the plays were received with the same enthusiasm with which they were produced. A unity rare in the theater existed between audience and actors. Each understood the other. This understanding bridged the gaps in production and glossed over the rough spots in the dialogue. The plays were mostly the sort of comedies or farces that have long runs in London's West End; but they brought back the tonic sound of men laughing together. This was a welcome contrast to the long months when the sullen silence was never broken except by snarls or complaints.

Two performances left an impression on me.

One was the "Dance of the Scarecrow." It was presented to us one night, without explanation or introduction. We did not know who the dancer was, but he must have been a tumbler or an acrobat, a London Music Hall performer, perhaps, of considerable gifts.

Dressed as a scarecrow, he tumbled about in time to the music, as though buffeted by the wind. His gymnastic dexterity was earning him unusually loud and prolonged applause.

A man in front of me leaned toward his neighbor and said in a low voice,

"Just like life, ain't it?"

The performer was more than an acrobat—he was an artist. Through the dance of the scarecrow, he was giving an artistic interpretation of man's condition that touched everyone in the audience. Sympathetic eyes followed every movement, every expression. They understood the message. The scarecrow's dancing suggested that while he was taking a beating, he wasn't going to give up and lie down. He would keep on going even though it hurt.

I listened again to the conversation in front of me.

"Reminds you of Charlie Chaplin, don't he?"

"Yes, the way he keeps getting knocked down, and then bobbing up again, as though coming back for more."

"Aye, he does that," said the first one. "He says to you that life *is* a knockabout, but you've got to keep going. It's the keeping going that makes him human, d'you see? Whenever he stops a bit, or lies down——he's just a scarecrow. Ain't that right?"

"Sure it is."

They watched the dance. Then the second man said,

"Queer, how he's got us all thinking the same thing, ain't it?"

"Yes, it is queer."

"Why do you s'pose that is?"

"I reckon somewhere along the line he's come to understand that's the way life is. And *we* understand that he understands."

"Yes," the second man said, "I reckon that's it."

The other performance that lingers in my memory was also a dance, although quite different in character. This was the "Dance of the Lotus Flower."

As the curtain went up, there was nothing to be seen but the lotus flower itself on the bare stage. To look at it one would never have dreamed that it was made from discarded rice sacks skillfully painted with homemade vegetable dyes and stretched on a bamboo frame.

The dancer was a Dutch Eurasian who had performed with a professional ballet company. This dance was his specialty.

The orchestra went into its overture. Slowly the lotus flower opened its petals. A lissome figure dressed from head to toe in black soared out and began to dance.

The shadow swept around the stage in a succession of

graceful arabesques. My comrades were following with rapt attention, interpreting every movement, each in his own way. By its sheer beauty, the dance reached into our minds and hearts to call forth memories and aspirations we had all but forgotten.

Delicately, the dancer painted for us a picture of hope.

"Yes, life is good," he seemed to be saying with his body. "Look at the beauty all around us. See it in the flower of which I am a part, in the sunlight which opens the petals and the breeze which moves me. I dance because I am a part of that beauty and because I am thankful for the mystery that is life."

He floated back into the lotus flower. The petals closed about him.

The orchestra faded out.

At irregular intervals there was community singing. We passed our requests to the master of ceremonies beforehand. Usually we asked for the songs of childhood. Among the favorites were "Tipperary," "Pack Up Your Troubles," "The Mountains of Mourne," "The Bonnie Banks of Loch Lomond," "Mother Machree," "Do Ye Ken John Peel?" and "Under the Spreading Chestnut Tree."

When the singing was at its height, the requests would shift to songs of a more inspirational character: "The Lord Is My Shepherd" (sung to the simple tune of Crimmond), "Abide with Me," "Jerusalem the Golden," and "Lead, Kindly Light."

The last chords ended, the prisoners, their spirits refreshed, moved back to their huts in a state of peace they had not known for a long time.

The leaven was spreading. We were spiritually armed. We had a will to life rather than a will to death.

But our weapons could be of little value unless we wielded them daily in the service of others. In that long dark period when we had lived by the law of the jungle intent only on our own survival, we had ignored the sick. We had regarded them as an offense. The very sight of them was a reproach, reminding us that they had left their share of the work to be done by the rest.

Although we wanted to help, it was not easy. The sick were so many, and those well enough to care for them were so few.

Since most of the illnesses stemmed from vitamin and protein deficiency, we tried to provide sustenance beyond the ration of rice. There was, of course, the canteen. But our pay was so meager that if we could buy a duck egg or a hand of bananas once a month we were doing well.

To extend our efforts, we took our chances by going outside the fence. Although to be caught meant death, prisoners undertook expeditions to procure food for their fellows.

We tried all sorts of experiments. We knew that fermentation produced vitamin B. So we let masses of rice ferment in water and used the liquid as medicine. The taste, however, was so vile that we couldn't induce our patients to drink it.

From a brew of this type, however, we learned to distill alcohol which proved invaluable to the doctors in sterilizing their instruments.

Down by the hospital we started a garden. It was small and inconspicuous, but it meant more to us than an acre of diamonds because there we transplanted any useful herb from the jungle.

With the help of two trained botanists, one an Englishman, the other Dutch, we were able to grow a number of plants of medicinal value. Most useful was one having strong narcotic effects which served as a substitute for anesthetics.

The botanists identified certain leaves, barks, and roots growing in the jungle which had therapeutic properties. One of these was a fruit about the size of an apple. It was evil-tasting and dark brown in color, but it afforded relief from dysentery.

Dinty Moore had brought me a supply during the early days when he was nursing me. The results from eating the fruit were immediate, curtailing my affliction so that I was able to enjoy a decent night's rest.

The task of our medical officers was a frustrating one. In spite of the limitations, however, they were able to do a marvelous work. They had to draw on all their resources. Never had the enemy Death been more powerful; never had the tools at their command been so limited.

Under these circumstances the practice of medicine was an art, rather than a science. Often when a surgeon was faced with a major operation, he had first to make his own instruments out of ordinary kitchen knives. Sutures were made from dried guts.

As alcohol became available for sterilizing and narcotics for anesthesia, the doctors were heartened and redoubled their efforts.

They trained some of us to give blood transfusions. The less sick gave their blood to the more sick, until the more sick became less sick and were able to give blood in turn. This became one of the most valuable services in the camp.

Of even greater importance than giving blood was the encouragement of patients to have faith in God. Faith strengthened their will to live. Without it, men died from no visible cause. With it, they survived a multiplicity of diseases, any one of which could have proved fatal.

We recovered respect for the dead.

When it became apparent that someone's end was near,

word would be passed around among his friends. Every effort would be made to see that there was a good turnout.

It was not possible to have a set time for funerals; the dead did not keep in that damp jungle heat; and men died at all hours. But no longer were they chucked into a common pit.

A group of friends gathered to form a funeral cortege, wearing, out of respect, either clean loincloths or shirts and shorts. They would march behind the pallbearers, carrying the deceased to his last resting place.

Later, when chaplains came to Chungkai, one of them would deliver a brief service. When no chaplain was on hand, an officer would read a passage from the Bible.

Every man went to a grave of his own, with a cross to mark it. On the cross a friend carved the pertinent facts of his life: his name, regiment and rank, and the dates of his birth and death.

An orderly method was worked out for disposing of a man's worldly goods. These were distributed among those closest to him in his unit.

Because human life had value once more, we also regained respect for ourselves. Stealing ceased; mutual confidence grew. It extended to the issuing of our daily rations. Our cooks did their best with little and our servers tried to be fair.

The first acts of our recovery had taken place under the worst of circumstances, at the very bottom of the abyss. Now there were many living examples of faith and courage among our fellow P.O.W.'s to hearten and inspire the rest of us. Among them was a young private from Aberdeen who had joined our battalion with the last draft. I remembered him vividly because of his high spirits. He always had a quip on his lips and an inexhaustible stock of jokes about his native city.

When I met him again at Chungkai he was no more than a shadow of his once sturdy self. He had heart disease, beriberi, malaria, and dysentery as well as a host of minor afflictions. The wonder was not so much that he was getting about but that he was alive at all.

Yet he was so busy he hardly had time to stop and talk. I learned that he was running a Bible lending library, one that he had thought of and organized himself. By barter, gift, and the fact of death he had accumulated a large store of Bibles. But his Bibles were in such great demand that he could loan them out for only an hour at a time. Jock took them around himself, collected them when the hour was up, and passed them on to the next on the waiting list. As he went, with his faith and humor, both of which were very great, he infused life into those whose spirits were flagging.

A day came when no Bibles were passed around. The patients wanted to know what had become of Jock. We learned that he had come down with cholera and had been taken to the isolation area. This was as good as the end. The cholera compound was a place from which few returned. He was mourned by the many to whom he had brought comfort and cheer. The library service was resumed, but there was no substitute for Jock's hearty voice and kindly manner.

One day he came back. Although he was so diseased there was hardly a healthy piece of flesh on him and so weak he could not stand, with his unquenchable spirit he had survived. He was bedridden now, but the place where he lay became a shrine for men to visit and come away strengthened. Their number was evidence of how much he was beloved.

I used to stop by to chat with him every morning on my way to work on the railroad. He always greeted me with a smile and a word of kindness. His concern was for me rather than for himself. It was the same for his comrades, whose stories he knew so well.

One morning when I asked him how he was feeling, he answered as usual,

"Oh, I'm not so bad, sir. I might be an awful lot worse. There's always something to thank God for. I enjoy life and I've got good friends. And it won't be so long before we'll be goin' home."

He gave me a reassuring smile as though I were the one who needed encouragement.

When I returned from work that evening I heard that within an hour after I left him Jock had died. His wasted body had found peace. But the memory of his gallant spirit remained. Jock had challenged us by his example in a way we would never forget.

CHAPTER 7

Church Without Walls

I DO NOT KNOW WHEN THE CHURCH AT CHUNGKAI was built. Perhaps "built" is not the right word, for it was no more than a clearing in the jungle. It had for a roof the great vault of the firmament and for its walls the forest of bamboo. There were no doors. One could enter at any point. It was all door.

It was hard to know when one was in church and when one was not. I remember watching two P.O.W.'s carrying a load of bamboo through the neighborhood. As they were jogging along, one of them called to the other, "Take your hat off, Joe, you're in the house of God."

The church was a fellowship of those who came in freedom and love, to acknowledge their weakness, to seek a presence, and to pray for their fellows. The Confession of Jesus Christ as Lord was the one requirement for membership. The church was made up of Methodists, Baptists, Episcopalians, Presbyterians, Congregationalists, and former agnostics.

Two Chinese were among those baptized. British troops found them still alive after a massacre on one of the beaches by the Japanese. The soldiers brought them back to Changi, dressed them in British uniforms, and equipped them with fictitious identities. They were absorbed into the life of the camp and had come on with us to Chungkai. Here they were so impressed by what they had seen and heard of the ex-

173

amples of their Christian fellows that they asked to be admitted to the church.

So far as most of us could see, there were three definitions of the church. There was the church composed of laws, practices, books, pews, pulpits, stones, and steeples; the church adorned with the paraphernalia of state. Then there was the church composed of creeds, catechisms, and theological professors, a church which was identified by words in great volume.

Finally, there was the church of the spirit, called out of the world to exist in it by reason of its joyful response to the initiative of God's love. Such a church had the atmosphere not of law court nor of classroom but of divine humanity. It existed wherever there was Christ's love. The physical temple and the doctrinal affirmation are needed—but both are dead without the church that is communion, the fellowship of God's people.

Ours was the church of the spirit. It was the throbbing heart which gave life to the camp and transformed it in considerable measure from a mass of frightened individuals into a community. From it we received the inspiration that made life possible. Such inspiration was not merely a rosy glow in the abdomen, but the literal inbreathing of the Holy Spirit that enabled men to live nobler lives, to become kind neighbors, to create improvements for the good of others, including such mundane matters as learning to cook better rice. The fruits of the Holy Spirit were clearly in evidence—"love, joy, long-suffering, gentleness, peace, goodness and faith."

At one end of the clearing prayerful hands had fashioned a Holy Table of bamboo on which were placed a cross and a lamp. The cross was a carved piece of wood; the lamp a tin can with a shoelace as a wick. A roof of atap palm protected them from the elements.

These symbols were meaningful ones to us. The Holy Table reminded us of the holy fellowship to which we belonged, a fellowship made possible by the sacrifice of Him who is Lord of the Church and by those who followed Him as apostles and disciples. Around the common table we gathered in visible evidence of His presence with us to heal, restore, and save. The cross pointed us to our heavenly Father and at the same time reached out its arms to include us all in an expression of the Love that will never let go.

As the lamp flickered in the tropical darkness to give us the only light we had for our service, it reminded us of the life that is "the light of men, the true light that enlightens every man who comes into the world," the light that never fails.

I did not become aware of the church's existence until the Rev. Alfred Webb arrived with a batch of prisoners from another camp. He began an effective ministry and quickly established himself as a wise and kindly pastor to an ever-increasing congregation. He heard of my discussion-group activities and graciously invited me to assist him.

The Sunday evening came when I was to preach my first sermon. There were no homiletic aids. But there was the Living Word, His testimony in the Bible, and His word for our condition. Shortly before the service was to begin, my friend Bill Maclean handed me his Bible. It was open at these words in the twelfth chapter of St. Luke:

"And when they bring you before the synagogues, and the rulers, and the authorities, be not anxious how or what ye shall answer or what ye shall say: for the Holy Spirit will teach you in that very hour what ye shall say."

Thus strengthened, I found the words. I preached on the parable of the prodigal son. Men came with ready hearts to the services, hearts open to receive the blessings God alone could give. Days later they would approach me to discuss a point of interest. The nature of their questions enlightened me, making it plain that the basic spiritual needs are common to all men.

A service at which prayers were said for the sick, for those at home, and for our daily needs was held every evening. We prayed for guidance and for strength to face the trials that lay ahead.

We needed the gift of a tranquil spirit, so we asked for an untroubled sleep. In the security of our civilian lives sleep was a matter to which we never gave much thought. But here it was different. Men's minds were troubled by the memory of horrors that permitted them no rest. Often their screams disturbed the sleeping camp.

I remember a fellow prisoner in my hut who was dying of cerebral malaria. As he turned and twisted on his pallet he carried on a conversation with an unseen presence. Apparently he had been ordered to kill a Malay, accused of being a spy, for security reasons. His conversation went something like this:

"Of course I had to kill him. There was nothing else to do. But before I shot him through the head he looked at me, his eyes pleading for mercy. I gave him no mercy when he asked for mercy. He cannot forgive me; his wife cannot forgive me; nobody can forgive me."

He went on for hours, arguing in this vein. As he reached the darkest depths of the valley he became quieter and then shouted out,

"But I am forgiven. You've given me peace."

He was at rest, and at rest he died.

It was to quiet ourselves, in the face of experiences such as these, that we joined in the closing prayer of the evening:

"O Lord, support us all the day long of this troublesome life, until the shadows lengthen and the evening comes and the busy world is hushed and the fever of life is over and our work is done. Then, Lord, in thy mercy grant us safe lodging, a holy rest, and peace at last; through Jesus Christ our Lord."

When we said the Lord's Prayer we stumbled over the phrase, "And forgive us our trespasses as we forgive those who trespass against us." This was not only because some us were of Scottish background, and accustomed to using "debts" and "debtors." It was because it meant asking forgiveness for the Japanese.

We had learned from our Bible reading that Jesus had his enemies just as we had ours. But there was this difference: He loved his enemies.

He prayed for them. Even as the nails were being hammered through his hands and feet, he cried out, "Father, forgive them, for they know not what they do."

We hated ours. We had spent a good deal of time in plotting for them a rich variety of satisfying punishments. We could see how wonderful it was that Jesus forgave in this way. Yet for us to do the same was beyond our attainment.

The first communion which I attended was memorable. With expectant hearts men had come to receive the strength that only God could give. The elements were of our daily life— rice baked into the form of bread, and fermented rice water. The solemn words of the fraction were said:

"Who the same night in which he was betrayed, took bread and when he had blessed, and given thanks, he brake it and said, Take, eat; this is my body which is broken for you; this do in remembrance of me."

We broke the bread as it was passed to us and then passed it to our neighbor.

The elements were returned to the Table, a prayer of Thanksgiving said, a hymn sung, and a blessing given. We slipped quietly away into the singing silence of the night, cherishing as we did so our experience of the communion of saints. The Holy

Spirit had made us one with our neighbors, one with those at home, one with the faithful in every land, in every age, one with the disciples.

All the while our own future was unpredictable. We didn't know what the Japanese might have in store for us. We had no assurance that we would ever again see home or those we loved.

But whatever happened, we knew that Jesus our leader would never fail us. As he had been faithful to his disciples in the first century, he would be faithful to us in the twentieth. In the words of John Masefield's play, he is "let loose in the world."

CHAPTER 8

Christmas Day, 1943

CHRISTMAS DAY WAS TO BE SOMETHING SPECIAL this year. With the completion of the railroad in November the Japanese had relaxed their pressure. The guards did not enter into our daily lives except for their irritating habit of patrolling through the camp and forcing us to bow to them when they appeared.

We were looking forward to the day, for the opportunity it would give us to express our feelings about the new insights we had gained. We only hoped the monsoon rains would not be falling as they had on Christmas last year.

I had been out of my shack for several weeks and was living with about two hundred others in the hut for those afflicted with amoebic dysentery. It was a kind of quarantine.

A few days before Christmas Dinty Moore came to visit me. I could tell from his manner that this was not a casual call.

After we had exchanged amenities, he said,

"I've come to get you all tickety-boo for Christmas."

"What do you have in mind?" I inquired cautiously.

"I'm going to shave off that magnificent beaver."

Sadly, I ruffled the luxuriant black growth in which I took pride.

"With what?"

"This."

179

He flourished a kitchen knife.

"Ground to a wafer edge."

He brought out a sliver of soap and a rag.

"Sit down," he said. "Let's have a go at it."

I sat on the edge of my sleeping platform while he worked the soap to a thin lather, and rubbed it into my whiskers.

He carved away my beard a patch at a time. The operation resembled some ancient Chinese torture. I was sure the skin was coming off with the whiskers. But so great was Dinty's pride in his talent and his homemade razor that I could only sit tight-lipped and say nothing.

He finished at last and handed me a mirror. He had left me a fine, bushy upswept mustache; otherwise, I was clean-shaven. Most of the skin, to my surprise, was intact.

"Now," beamed Dinty, contemplating his handiwork, "you're ready to celebrate."

Christmas Day dawned. To my joy I saw brilliant blue skies overhead. Already we had one welcome gift, that of glorious weather.

I looked down the hut. It was hardly recognizable. The ground was clean and neatly swept. The bamboo bed slats had been taken out and thoroughly debugged. The walls above the sleeping platforms were garlanded with green boughs —the one note of Christmas cheer the jungle offered in abundance. Men stirred, got up, and began to move about, wishing each other a hearty "Merry Christmas."

For once we ate our breakfast in leisurely, gentlemanly fashion. Then we prepared for church. We wore whatever was our best, although it may have been no more than a clean loin-cloth.

I went early to church. I wanted to have a few moments of quiet. Someone had made a Christmas wreath of jungle greens.

Resting against the ivory-colored bamboo of the Holy Table, it gave a feeling of serenity.

Others had also come for those moments of hallowed quiet. Men entered softly. By fifteen minutes before eleven o'clock, when the service was to begin, the church was full. Some were sitting on the ground, some on bamboo benches, some on homemade stools. But most were standing along the sides and at the back or front, whichever one might like to call it. Over two thousand P.O.W.'s filled the area. But the hush I had felt when I first arrived remained unbroken.

Padre Webb entered and took his place in front of the Holy Table. He prayed in silence, raised his head and announced the first hymn, "O come, all ye faithful, joyful and triumphant, O come ye, O come ye to Bethlehem." He did not need to say the words and have us repeat them after him. Those who knew them sang them; those who did not picked them up from their neighbor.

Bill Maclean was standing beside me. He was singing bass and in Latin. We had been at St. Andrews University together. While we sang, there came to my mind the going-down service before our last Christmas at home, which both of us had attended. I could see the scarlet-robed students and the yellow lights of the lanterns, making a warm Christmas-card picture against the old gray walls of the university chapel.

We sang a second carol, "Noel, Noel." Padre Webb gave a brief sermon. His topic was "The Hope of Christmas." We came to the closing hymn, "Good Christian Men, Rejoice."

While we were singing we heard the almost-forgotten wail of the air-raid siren. It rose, then gradually died away. Far off we could hear the rumble of a plane. We exchanged glances. This could not be Japanese. We kept on singing. In the blue sky over our heads we heard a four-engine bomber flying confidently in the direction of Bangkok. We put all our feeling

into that hymn. More lustily than ever we sang "Rejoice!"
Indeed we sang so lustily that the prison guards came charging
into the church, shouting the Japanese equivalent of "Shut
up! They'll hear you."

I had known of the power of praise. But I was not aware
that it could soar ten to fifteen thousand feet and be picked up
by a bomber crew above the engine noise.

The padre pronounced the benediction and sent us forth
in peace.

We were barely out of the church area when someone
slapped me on the back.

"Merry Christmas, Merry Christmas, Ernie old boy!"

It was Bill Maclean, wearing an enormous smile.

"You must have been thinking the same thoughts as myself,"
I said.

"You mean—that plane was a symbol of hope?"

I changed my pace to keep step with his, and said,

"Yes. I wonder if the crew have any idea what they mean to
us. Poor blighters. They're no doubt grumpy because they have
to fly out of their billet on Christmas Day."

"Probably a U.S.A.F. plane taking photographs. I hope
they saw us."

"If they didn't see us," I replied, "perhaps they heard us
after all."

The happy looks on the faces of the men walking near us
and the loud hum of their conversation as they returned to
their huts and their Christmas dinners indicated they were all
having the same reaction.

I remarked to Bill,

"This *is* a Merry Christmas—especially when you compare
it to last year."

"Last year!" He made a face. "That was a muddy mess. No
holiday, no church service, hardly any food. If I remember
correctly, you couldn't eat anything anyway."

"Right. I was on a diet of nothing. That was just before I got 'dip' and a few other things. It was almost the end."

Bill looked more serious.

"We're not out of the woods yet—not by a long way. But now there's hope. That's the thing—there's hope."

At our hut a Lancashire artillery captain welcomed us with the confidential air of one letting us in on a big secret.

"Back from your prayers, are you? Now that you've filled your souls you can fill your bellies. We're going to have a whopping dinner! Soup made from meat and bones! Rissoles with meat in them—rice and a slice of old Thai cow. And— to top it off—Christmas pudding!"

"Who're you kidding!" Bill and I chorused.

"Tell us more," I begged.

"You know that cook we've got in the kitchen?" the gunner said. "The one who used to be some kind of technician in Blighty? The one who claims all you need to cook properly is intelligence?"

"Sure."

"Well, he's invented Christmas pudding made from rice. First he boils it, and leaves it to ferment along with bananas, limes, and palm sugar, then steams it. Wait till you taste it!"

We went to fetch our mess tins. We wanted to be sure to be in line at the serving rack outside the hut when the dinner arrived, to savor this miracle for ourselves.

It was the first decent meal we'd had in two years. The ration of meat was small by normal standards but lavish by those of Chungkai.

I ate slowly, enjoying each mouthful and the festive atmosphere. Then came the pudding. It was delicious. In fact, it was so good that I decided to keep mine to share with Dusty and Dinty who were coming to visit me that evening.

In the afternoon there was a Christmas pantomime. It was largely inspired nonsense, something called "Snow White and the Seven Dwarfs," with our guards as the villains and Snow White as the spirit of innocence. The Japanese, who were self-invited guests, had no notion that they were the butt of the jokes, and laughed and applauded with the rest of us.

In the evening P.O.W.'s went from hut to hut, taking Christmas presents to the men who could not leave their beds. These gifts, which showed both variety and craftsmanship, they had made themselves from whatever materials were available. Out of hides from the slaughterhouse they had fashioned pouches which could be hung from a G-string to carry personal possessions. They had also made wallets, razor strops, book markers, or protective covers for Bibles. From the plentiful bamboo they had created many mementoes ranging from carved and decorated mess bowls to simple remembrance plaques inscribed "Merry Christmas, Chungkai, 1943."

Most of us in the amoebic dysentery hut had made our own open lamps from beaten tin cans, and had pooled our slender resources to buy a small supply of coconut oil. Ordinarily we were niggardly with our light. But tonight we forgot economy and basked in the glow from not one, but two lamps.

Sitting with me as we talked over the events of the day were Bill Maclean, "Ginger" (Alastair) Ross, another Argyll, and a small, slight cockney officer, who was called The Mighty Atom because of his irrepressible impudence.

The Mighty Atom looked around him and rubbed his hands in anticipation, raising his left eyebrow and crooking his elbow by placing his left hand on his knee. This posture gave him a cheeky look as he prepared to disclose *his* secret. He leaned forward.

"Ginger's bummed some alcohol. That's what he's done—he's bummed some dear old, sweet old alc—the food of rakes and kings."

"How?" asked Bill.

"Simple," said The Mighty Atom with a puckish leer. "He's a bloody vampire, that's what he is."

Ginger was in charge of the blood transfusion service.

"All he did was sell a pint of somebody else's blood for an ounce of the water of life—and a fair trade at that."

"I did nothing of the sort, you Sassenach sod," Ginger laughed. "I merely reminded the bloke who runs the still that we were buddies.

"Fancy anyone wanting to be a buddy of yours!" jeered The Mighty Atom with a wink.

"Oh, shut up," said Ginger.

With a triumphant flourish he produced a can covered with a piece of rag. The Mighty Atom was handing mugs around when a voice broke in,

"Just in time for the party."

Dusty and Dinty had arrived. I introduced them to the others. They moved in on either side of me to join the circle gathered around the two lamps and the can of rice alcohol.

"While you're fixing the gut-and-brain rot I'll give the lads something I have for them," I said.

I fumbled in my pack, brought out the Christmas pudding which I had saved, and divided it in two.

"Here's something to wish on." I handed each a small portion. "And here's your Christmas." I gave them each two duck eggs, a hand of bananas, and two bahts.

Their faces, in the warm light of the lamps, showed astonished pleasure.

"This is the richness, thank you," said Dinty.

"I hardly know what to say," stammered Dusty. "It's been some Christmas."

Meanwhile, Ginger and The Mighty Atom had mixed a brew of alcohol, lime juice, and palm sugar. They served our guests first in two borrowed mugs. Ginger, having provided the spirit, was given the honor of proposing the toast. He became solemn.

"Well, chaps," he said, "I'm not given much to talking like Ernie here. What I want to say is that I hope all our Christmas wishes come true."

We raised our mugs and drank.

Dusty turned his fine face in my direction. In his quiet, gentle voice he said,

"Quite a difference, isn't there, between the way the year is ending and the way it began?" He spoke more slowly and more definitely. "Then, none of us thought you'd live."

I smiled to ease the emotion he was feeling, and said,

"Well, you can see for yourself how wrong you were. It's only thanks to you and Dinty and others like you that I'm here . . . So you really thought I wouldn't make it!"

"To tell the truth," said Dusty, "I didn't see how on earth you possibly could." Then he added shyly, "But I prayed that you would."

After our taste of Christmas cheer, we had a mug of hot coffee made from sweetened burned rice. That finished, we sat holding our empty mugs, fascinated by the brave flames of our little lamps. They sputtered and sighed, but they kept going. Ginger and The Mighty Atom were smoking foul-smelling cigarettes made from split paper and coarse rank tobacco grown locally for the manufacture of nicotine.

Ginger took a last puff and said,

"About time for 'Lights out.' Let's close with 'Auld Lang Syne.' "

There was no need to assent. His suggestion suited our mood. We gazed at the flames and with soft voices sang,

> *"For auld lang syne, my dear*
> *For auld lang syne*
> *We'll tak' a cup of kindness yet*
> *For auld lang syne."*

We broke up and blew out the lamps. In the darkness of the hut we wished Dusty and Dinty many happy Christmases. When Dinty shook hands, he said,

"It's been a good evening." Then he reminded me,

"This has been our first reunion. Here's hoping we have a lot more like it."

I walked them to the door and watched them merge into the black tropic night.

Just then the bugle wailed its sad good-by to the day. Christmas for that year of 1943 was over.

CHAPTER 9

On from Chungkai

CHRISTMAS WAS THE HIGH POINT. FROM THAT time on, conditions in the camp went rapidly downhill.

The Railroad of Death had long since been finished. The originally estimated five- to six-year project that was to have been completed in eighteen months had taken only twelve. But the toll in suffering endured and lives lost was fantastic. The railroad was two hundred and fifty miles long. Every mile of it cost, on an average, the lives of sixty-four prisoners of war and two hundred and forty Southeast Asians.

A prick of conscience must have been felt somewhere, for a report on the appalling conditions under which we had been forced to work eventually reached Tojo. The only action taken, however, was to select one camp commandant as a scapegoat and to court-martial him for the sins of all his colleagues. At the Tokyo Tribunal, it was declared that this action only condoned the crimes.

After the war the railroad was sold to the Thais by the British Government for six million dollars. Later the rails were torn up. The jungle did the rest.

While we were still at Chungkai we heard a rumor that the Japanese were planning to erect a memorial to our dead at Tamarkan. But they had already done that; there was the railroad.

The camps upcountry began to empty. The P.O.W.'s who were left alive came trudging back to Chungkai at all hours of the day and night. A few of their faces still showed signs of life; but many were expressionless. The inner spark had been quenched. They had come here to die. Many had no recognizable disease that doctors could treat in any way. They had lost their hold on life, and despair had destroyed the self. Aimlessly, they shuffled along in a gray, twilight existence, waiting for death.

Chungkai had become a transit camp to hold survivors until another project could be found to use their wornout bodies. They came in such numbers and there was so little we could do to help them that at first we were overwhelmed. We tried every means to reach them, but their faces betrayed no reaction to tell us we were succeeding. They seemed to have no center left from which to hear and respond. Food meant nothing to them. The canned milk and other luxuries which we obtained for them on the black market could not tempt them. Their appetites were gone.

They were isolated from life. Talking to them of home evoked no memories, for memory had been obliterated by fear. With memory had vanished their identity as human beings. They had been killed in a way more fiendish than physical torture. They were dead before they stopped breathing.

But we rejected despair. We visited all new groups as they came in to see what we could do. This was a haunting experience, for we never knew when we would encounter missing friends or old service companions.

Once, as I passed down the sleeping platforms in a hut filled with fresh arrivals, a hand came out and gripped me. A voice said,

"Excuse me, sir, aren't you Ernie Gordon who used to be in the Gourock Boy Scouts with me?" I recognized Ian Car-

ruthers, a friend of my boyhood on the Firth of Clyde. I had
not seen him since those days. He had an ugly jungle ulcer
on his leg, but aside from that he was not so badly off as
some. We had many a blether about old times while he was
with us in the camp.

In another group I met an old service companion of mine,
Sergeant MacKay, who had been captured in the jungle after
the battle of Slim River in the Malayan campaign. He had a
present for me.

At one point he had been sent on a work party to Port
Dickson, where most of our personal baggage remained before
we went into action. The Japanese had taken our belongings,
with the exception of one garment, of which they couldn't
make head or tail—that was the kilt. They allowed the
P.O.W.'s to have their pick and Sergeant MacKay recognized
mine by its unusual panel design; it had been given me by a
friend who had had it from World War I. He had carried that
kilt of mine from camp to camp, hoping to find me.

At the end of February the Japanese disclosed that
Chungkai was to be disbanded. Its able-bodied occupants
would be sent to work in Japan. Parties were formed, equipped
with warm clothing, and dispatched to Singapore for embarkation.

Afterward, at our liberation, we heard what had happened
to them. They were transported in old hulks bought by the
Japanese in the depression years. Ships that had been built on
the Clyde and sailed with pride on the seven seas became the
tombs of the sons of the fathers who had built them.

Prisoners of war were packed into the holds, not like cattle
but like coal. There was almost no ventilation, no food, very
little water, and no sanitation. They were stacked on sleeping
platforms built three feet above one another, the space allowed
being six feet by six feet for each fifteen men. Thus confined
they had to sit cross-legged for the duration of the voyage.

Once at sea the hatches were closed and they were left to stew in their own juices.

The ships displayed no red crosses to show that they were carrying P.O.W.'s. In consequence, a number of them were torpedoed by American submarines. In this way died many of our friends. Thus died Ian Carruthers.

Thus died Dinty (Dennis Joseph) Moore.

Chungkai, too, was dying. It was almost half empty when I was ordered to join a party being sent to a camp for convalescents at Nakawm Paton. This was supposed to be a model camp, built according to Red Cross specifications. But we looked forward to it with little enthusiasm, since we took it to be just another of their empty promises.

While we were waiting to leave Chungkai, Ginger Ross came running into our hut in a high state of excitement.

"Guess what!" he said breathlessly. "Mail is being given out tomorrow."

Mail! It was not possible. In all the interminable months since I had made my escape from Singapore I had received only one communication from the world outside. That was a cablegram of greeting from a friend of mine in Chungking, China, who was Far Eastern representative for U.S. Steel. How or why it got through I will never know. But as to what was happening at home I'd had not a word.

"How do you know?" I asked skeptically.

"I have it straight from the horse's mouth!" said Ginger excitedly. "Right from the lads at H.Q. There's a ruddy great pile of it. They've already sorted it according to huts."

A troubling thought crossed my mind.

"But what if there aren't letters for everybody? That would be awful."

"Oh, there will be," said Ginger confidently. "Or almost everybody. They tell me there are great masses of them."

I had difficulty falling asleep that night. When I slept I dreamed of the letters that had come for me. I could see so clearly the blue envelopes addressed in my father's distinctively bold handwriting. There would be letters from my mother telling me about life at home, about what my brother, my sister, and my friends were doing. At the end of each letter would be added a cheerful note from my dad, expressing his characteristic optimism. These letters were so real in my dreams that I never questioned whether I would receive them or not. I knew that I would.

We waited impatiently all through the next day. Then, a little before suppertime, there was a triumphant cry of "Mail up!"

Ginger had been right. At the entrance to the hut were the boys from H.Q. with bags of mail. Everyone rushed to the doorway. Everyone, that is, except me. I walked over calmly with the assurance that my letters awaited my coming.

I stood at the back of the crowd and listened to the names being called out one by one. It pleased me to see the happiness on the faces of my hutmates as they went away, clutching their envelopes. The mail was being handed out in alphabetical order. The G's had been called. I did not hear my name. Then came the H's, the I's, the J's, the K's, the L's, and the M's. The mail stack was dwindling. I waited, certain that mine had been misplaced. The S's were called, the T's, and the W's. A few still waited; and only a letter or two was left. Then there were none.

The officer who was making the distribution looked up as he gathered together the empty mail sacks and saw me standing alone.

"Sorry, Ernie, old boy," he said sympathetically. "Now that this load got through, we're sure to have another one soon. There'll be some for you then."

"Why certainly," I replied as cheerfully as I could.

I walked back to my bed space as slowly as I had come.

One morning a trainload of empty cars stopped on its way back from Burma to Bangkok. With surprisingly little fuss we were paraded and entrained. Although Nakawm Paton was no great distance, it took us a day and a night to reach it.

At first sight, it appeared better than we had expected. The long huts had been well-constructed and laid out in blocks. There were even some buildings made of brick and cement. These were the cookhouses. Our sleeping platforms, stretching along the sides of the huts in rows as in Chungkai, were of planking rather than of split bamboo.

We were seeking our billets, feeling rather pleased with what we had seen, when nearby we heard a deafening roar. A flight of fighter planes was streaking into the air from a concrete strip alongside the camp. They circled overhead, climbed into the clouds, and were lost to sight.

Then we knew. The camp had been laid out this way so that it would be clearly recognizable from the air for what it was. Quite rightly, the Japanese assumed that our fliers would not drop bombs on their own. This gave their fighters a chance to take to the air unmolested.

Nakawm Paton was essentially a camp for the sick, filled with those who had been crushed by too much work, by disease, by too little food and too many unkindnesses, the flotsam and jetsam from all the camps along the railroad.

So many were sick that they were segregated according to illness. One hut was reserved exclusively for tropical ulcer cases; another for those with beriberi; still another for victims of amoebic dysentery.

One hut was surrounded by a high wire fence. Here were the men who had broken and gone insane. They roamed about in their cage, twisting their hands and making strange guttural noises and staring out at us with frightened eyes. The Japanese were afraid to go near them and had appointed special orderlies from among the P.O.W.'s to minister to their needs. These were the first men I had encountered whom captivity had driven mad. I marveled that there were so few.

Farther away, behind a similar barricade, was another, smaller colony. They were lepers. Their food was dropped to them over the wire by means of long bamboo poles.

An atmosphere of listlessness prevailed at Nakawm Paton. The men had been taken from their regimental groups, from the companionship of their friends, to be sent here; hence there was a total lack of community.

In some ways, however, conditions were better than those at Chungkai. There was no back-breaking toil: the only work to be done was that of running the camp. The rations were slightly improved.

The administration of the camp was under the direction of a British medical officer. There was also on the staff a gifted Australian brain surgeon, Lt. Col. A. E. Coates, who had passed through our escape route on the Indragiri and had been taken prisoner at Padang.

Colonel Coates performed wonders of surgery every day. He had discovered among the prisoners a maker of scientific instruments, who, under his guidance, fashioned a wide array of them for special operations. For the most part, Colonel Coates had to operate without anesthetics, although from time to time he was able to coax some from the visiting Japanese staff doctor when the latter stopped to admire his work.

At this camp we had no such reservoir of talent as at Chungkai. But there were some things we could do—or at least try to do. We could make an effort to put these bedridden, hopeless men back on their feet and arouse in them a desire to live.

Here, as at Chungkai, Ginger Ross and The Mighty Atom organized their blood transfusion service.

Next, we formed a team of masseurs and went to work. But

we found our patients at Nakawm Paton did not want to walk. They did not wish to live.

Our first job was to help them find a reason for living. This involved the stirring of memories which they had long buried in their subconscious in order to make existence endurable. As we rubbed their muscles we talked of home and friends. This must have been as painful to them as it was for them to walk again on their matchstick legs.

One hard case was a young farmer from Norfolk, in the east of England. I found him lying on his rack, dirty, paralyzed, weak, without hope. I affected a hearty, confident manner and introduced myself.

"Here I am," I said. "I've come to help you walk again."

Slowly, very slowly, he looked up at me with pathetic eyes. He spoke with a dialect so thick that I could barely understand him.

" 'Taint any use."

"Why do you say that?"

"I can't walk. I'll never be able to walk."

"Why not?"

" 'Cause I can't, that's why. And 'taint much good you tryin' to help me any."

His tone suggested annoyance.

"What do you want me to do?" I asked somewhat sharply. "Leave you alone to rot in your misery?"

"Might as well. 'Taint any point in walkin'. 'Taint any point in livin'."

He turned his face from me.

"Away with you!" I said with a lightness I did not feel. "There must be someone worth remembering. Haven't you anyone—a mother, a father, a sweetheart?"

I looked down at him. He was not a pretty sight.

"I'll bet a good-looking man like you must have been a riot with the lassies."

No response, not even a wan smile.

"I'll bet you're even married."

"Aye, that I am. And I've a nipper I've never seen. But 'taint any good. There's too much sufferin' and too much trouble for anything good to survive. We're licked. We're all licked. The Japs will kill us all. Nothin' good can happen."

He stared up at me in misery.

"The Jerries will have bombed my wife and baby by this time."

I had to quiet this fear. I told him I heard the war in Europe wasn't going as badly as all that.

"Let's get started," I urged. "The massage certainly can't harm you and it might do you some good. There isn't too much wrong with you. You've had beriberi, but not very badly. Now you're getting better. You have lost the ability to walk. But all we have to do is to get it back."

Grudgingly, he permitted me to massage him. Day by day, as I worked on his useless legs, I kept up much the same kind of conversation.

"Have you ever thought how lucky you are?" I asked him. "You've got a wife and son to go back to. You're ahead of most of us."

"It's like I said before," he insisted. "How can I know I've got a home left? Jerries might have blown it up. There's been no word to say they ain't."

"And there's been no word to say they have," I replied. "Is that what you're afraid of? Or are you worried that your wife is running around with someone else? One of those damn Yanks, for instance; or a Pole?"

"No, I ain't scared of that. My wife's a good woman. She's a teacher, a primary teacher, and she's savin' her pay so that I can buy into my brother-in-law's business. He's a grain merchant."

"Sound's pretty good to me," I said. "But while she's working hard building a future for both of you, you're rejecting it.

You don't want it. You want to die. Doesn't seem quite fair to me, from what you've told me."

He made no reply.

"Are you scared to go back in case you don't like her any more? You've forgotten what she looks like, I bet."

"No! No! 'Taint it!" he burst out. "She's right pretty, that's what she is. If I'd been able to keep my picture wallet, I'd show you how pretty she is. But the Japs took it off me."

"Give me a word picture, then. Does she have pink eyes? Is her nose flat or what?"

He answered angrily,

"No, her eyes ain't pink. They're gray. And her nose ain't flat, it's straight. She dresses nicely, too, my wife does. Knows how to use a bit of color, and how to do her hair up right pretty."

"Can you see her?" I asked.

"'Course I can see her. It's as if she was standin' here before me."

"Isn't it as I said—you are luckier than most of us!"

A faint smile almost appeared on his face. He began to be interested.

"Now you're feelin' sorry for yourself instead of me," he said with a certain amount of pleasure.

"Indeed I am. And why not? There's no lass saving up her pay for me. Any girl friends I had will have been married by this time. With all the foreign troops stationed in Britain there won't be a girl left for any of us by the time this war is over."

He smiled a little and I continued,

"Besides, you've got a son waiting for you. You'll be a proper hero to him."

He raised himself on one elbow to listen more carefully.

"Dads always are heroes to their sons," I said, "but *he'll* have the satisfaction of knowing you are one. Quite a romantic figure you're going to cut when you come marching home

again. You'll be slim, all right—the Japs have seen to that—
and handsome, and you'll have plenty of ribbons to decorate
your manly chest."

I went on, giving him a portrait of himself that he could
see and take a liking to.

"You won't be so badly off yourself," he said, coming back
at me. "A gentleman like you should do very well after the
war."

"I'm not a gentleman," I said. "To be a gentleman, you need
an income of at least a thousand quid a year. No, I don't
qualify. I'll have to go to work."

"What will you do, then?"

"Well"—I hesitated. "I've thought I might buy a fishing
boat with my gratuity and go into the smuggling business, running brandy and scent from France to England. Or," I mused,
"I might get a job with the Scottish Nationalist Party, become
Commander-in-Chief of the Scottish Army, fight the Battle
of Bannockburn all over again, give you English the hiding of
your lives, and move the King back into Holyrood."

"We'd outnumber you ten to one," he answered.

"Ten Englishmen to one Scot? Why, that leaves the odds
in our favor."

"How do you figure that?"

"It's all a matter of diet: Scottish oatmeal porridge, the
Shorter Catechism, and Gumption Pie. Try it when you get
back. You'll be head of the grain business in no time."

"And I'll be waitin' to pull your leg as you're pullin' mine
now," he said with a chuckle.

At last I had brought him around to a more optimistic point
of view. We looked forward to our massage and conversational
sessions, but the time came when I had to encourage him to
do a little bit more.

One day I said to him,

"Well, I think I've done about everything that I can for

you. I can stop your massage and go on to someone else."

"Why?" he asked in bewilderment.

"What's the use? You'll never be able to walk again."

He perked up.

"Who said I wouldn't?"

"You did. Lying right here. Don't you remember?"

"Well, I've changed my mind. Mebbe I *will* be able to walk —if you'll help me."

He glanced at me hopefully.

"Do you still think we're licked?" I asked. "That trouble and suffering and death have the last word?"

"No, I don't think I do any more. Mebbe there are things that can survive this camp—and the war."

"Like what?"

"That I can't rightly say. I can't very well put it into words. I have a feelin' about it, you might say."

"Things like—faith, hope, and love, maybe?"

"Yes, yes—that's the sort of thing I mean. Faith, hope, and love, and things like them. I should've thought of them before, but I never did. Can't make out why."

"Then you must think there's something to live for."

"I reckon I do. I see that mebbe there is."

"Now you're getting somewhere," I said. "The message of Easter is that God isn't defeated and neither are the riches of His Spirit. Love, heroism, faithfulness, loyalty, love of beauty, respect for truth, and other things like that can't be chucked out on the refuse heap. They endure—when everything else is gone."

Slowly he answered,

"That sounds pretty good to me. Why did nobody never tell me that before?"

"Maybe they did, but maybe you weren't listening. Sometimes we hear only what we want to hear. One of the good things about this mess is that it is opening our eyes and our ears. When God speaks, He doesn't do so from the storm or the whirlwind, but from the silence with a still, small voice. But that's enough to keep you thinking for a while."

I gave his legs a final slap.

"Now get up on your feet!"

He looked startled.

"What's that you say?"

"You heard me!" I replied. "Up on your feet with you."

He did not move.

"You want to walk, don't you? Well, that's something you can't do lying on your back. Get up!"

He saw that I meant business. Without any further fuss he did his best to obey my command. Guiding his legs with his hands, he put his feet over the edge of the bamboo rack and placed them on the ground. Then he tried to raise himself with his hands. His legs wobbled under him like macaroni. He sank back.

"It's hopeless," he said in a dispirited voice.

I had to admit to myself that it appeared that way. But I did not let him know how I felt.

"No it isn't," I reassured him. "Here, let me give you a hand."

Taking his arm and putting it across my shoulder, I raised him to his feet. Most of his weight was borne by me. But for the first time in months he was standing—even if just barely. He lurched forward. Had he moved one leg? I couldn't tell. But I pretended that he had.

"You've taken a step!" I exclaimed.

He did not reply.

"There's an old Chinese proverb," I went on, "which says, 'The longest journey begins with but a single step.' That's what you've done. You've begun a journey."

I held him upright for a while and eased a little more of his weight onto himself. After a time he gasped,

"I've had enough. Let me down."

His face was contorted. He was unable to speak. He gazed at me with eyes that were almost pleading.

"Do you think—that I'll ever—be able—to stand on my own?"

"Of course you will," I said. "And you'll walk on your own, too. It will be a painful business at times. You've got to make up your mind to that. But I'll have you walking within a month. I'll lay you odds to that."

He was still skeptical.

"Tell you what. I'll bring you a walking stick tomorrow. Then you'll be able to help yourself a little more."

At that he cheered up a bit.

My estimate of a month proved optimistic. But not for want of trying. Every day I spent at least two hours with him. More often than not he was so depressed that he wanted to quit.

His reviving leg muscles pained him acutely. He complained that he could not sleep at night. I reassured him by explaining that this was a healthy sign—a sign of returning life. But he didn't believe me.

At last we reached the stage where he was ready to make an attempt at walking by himself with the support of a cane. He set out, moving rigidly, like an automaton. I followed behind, prepared to catch him. With his thigh muscles he raised the lower leg so that he could take a step. Then he let it fall and threw his weight forward so that he would be in position to do the same with his other leg.

As he made his precarious journey down the hut, all eyes were on him. Others lying on their sleeping platforms were identifying themselves with him. He was a symbol of their hopes. If he could do this, why not they?

One day, after he had made it for about two hundred yards, I said to him,

"Now you're on your own. I'm taking your cane. Keep walking."

Without any protest he handed me his staff.

Alone, he took a faltering step—another step—then another. He was walking. From that ragged crowd of watching men a cheer went up.

I saw he was near collapse. I ran to catch him. But at that precise moment he heard the cheer. He recovered his balance, threw back his shoulders, and stepped forward, walking with confident precision until I told him to stop.

He sat down. Sweat poured from his face, but he was grinning.

"I've done it, by gum!" he said happily. "I've done it!"

The recovery of the Norfolk farmer meant a great deal, not only to him, but to his hutmates. Through my fairly long association with him, I had come to know the others quite well. They had listened to our discussions and from time to time joined in.

Gradually I noticed that a few of them had started coming to our church services—a few at first, then more. I could pick them out, sitting together as a block. When I remarked that I was happy to see them there, one of them replied,

"We weren't too sure about it at first—seeing that we weren't the churchgoing type. But it seemed the right thing to do. Now it's becoming a habit or something, for we like it." With an affirmative bob of the head he added, "Yes, sir, we wouldn't miss it for nothing now—me and me mates."

The hut improved remarkably in appearance. When I first visited there it had been squalid. Although recently built it had quickly degenerated into a slum, redolent with the old smells of corruption, unwashed bodies, bedbugs, and open sores. Now I noticed a change. The planks that served as sleeping platforms were taken out, washed down, and left to dry in the sun to get rid of the vermin. The hut had been swept. Perhaps this persistent fight against dirt and the bed-bugs was the most significant indication of a reviving spirit.

Some attempts were made at decoration. There were no pictures of pin-up girls; the starvation diet had taken care of the sex urge. Instead there were pictures of apple pies, roast beef and potatoes, boxes of candy, steak and kidney pies, or chocolate cakes, all clipped from prewar magazines that had come our way. I shared with others a clipping I had found in an old American newspaper containing a recipe for angel food cake. It began with these choice words: "Take the whites of twelve eggs. . . ." We took pleasure in reading it aloud.

Men began to help one another. In the same pattern as Chungkai the less sick cared for the more sick. The few who could walk fetched water from the well in bamboo buckets and with good-natured banter began to wash those who were unable to wash themselves.

I realized I was seeing the same saving grace at work here that had redeemed us at Chungkai. In some ways the change taking place at Nakawm Paton was even more miraculous. Since this was a hospital camp, the hopelessness had been acute. Indeed, it had been so complete that men did not trouble to steal from each other. So many had wanted to do nothing but die. Now there was a stirring of hope, and with hope, the feeling that life was worth living.

Chungkai had been the training ground for the task of regenerating such camps as this. I never knew how many men had gone out from there to implement elsewhere what they learned. But there must have been scores of them.

Those who were dying—or thought they were—failed the more rapidly because they no longer wanted to eat. We made every effort, therefore, to tempt their lost appetites with something out of the ordinary.

A metal worker had devised a crude eggbeater out of a tin can and a perforated lid attached to a wooden plunger. One of our cooks had invented a confection of mashed bananas, duck eggs, and lime juice. Whipped to a creamy froth with the homemade eggbeater and poured over a bowl of rice, the mixture was a tasty dish.

When first offered, patients usually rejected it. Then we'd say,

"Oh, come on. Old Jim got this up especially for you. You wouldn't want to disappoint him, would you?"

The thought that someone had gone to so much trouble for them was often more of a turning point than the dish itself.

Faith sustained us as individuals, but it also sustained the community of which we were a part. It shaped our culture, determined our morality, and gave unity to our common life. It would be absurd to say that faith and reason were separated; for faith led to reflection and reflection involved reason. Men who had very little education developed a keen interest in a variety of subjects such as philosophy, politics, literature, law, and the humanities. Faith had inspired them to think creatively, to be aware of themselves, to be conscious of the ultimates, to be open to the world beyond their environment.

As at Chungkai, we saw men hungering for food for their minds as well as for their bodies. We tried, therefore, to start a university again. But we were handicapped by a lack of the trained scholars we'd had at the larger camp. I had been able to smuggle in some scraps of paper on which I had written down the Greek grammar I was endeavoring to compile. With the aid of these and what I could remember we began sessions in Greek and also in ethics and philosophy.

Since we were unable to provide courses on any extensive scale, and since the hunger for knowledge was so intense, we organized a "make-do" program enlisting whatever talent we could find.

Debating teams were formed with two on each side. They made the rounds of the huts, disputing on assigned topics. A favorite was: "Has twentieth-century man lost the ability to entertain himself?" Another: "Resolved: That old-age pensions should begin at twenty-one." When the debaters grew bored they switched sides and presented the opposite view with equal gusto.

On one of the teams was a debonair Londoner with a promising future as a barrister. He had an electric personality and a gift of eloquence. One night he came to me with an idea: Why not tell stories of famous trials? He gave a sample performance and proved to be a hit. So great was his skill as an actor that as he stood before us in his loincloth we could see him in our mind's eye in wig and gown, addressing the bench.

Any talent was put to use. One prisoner gave popular lectures on "The scientific approach to golf." An architect conducted a course on "How to design a house." The kitchen and the bathroom were the two rooms in which everyone showed the greatest interest.

Many were fascinated by the sea. Some designed yachts which they could never hope to own, or attended classes in how to build and sail a small boat. Once I recounted my adventures on the *Setia Berganti* to a group in my hut. The word got around and I was asked to tell it over and over to others.

The men also enjoyed listening to selections read from books. They liked simple tales that evoked nostalgic pictures of living in other times. Among the most popular were the tales of Washington Irving, especially "The Legend of Sleepy Hollow" and "Rip van Winkle."

The more men heard about the problems, foibles, quirks,

eccentricities, humors, and virtues of other people, the more they regained interest in the human race and in themselves. The evening reading sessions became increasingly popular. As I read, I sat on the edge of a sleeping platform, holding my book close to the lamp and giving as much feeling to the words as I could muster. The words conveyed pictures—of home, of families gathered around the parlor fire.

When I had finished my story for the night I was aware of a sense of kinship. We were human beings with the same puzzlements and the same hopes. We were being drawn toward a center that was beyond ourselves, a center that was good, that gave us cause to hope, that promised the fulfillment of life—a life that was joyously sweet.

One evening I observed to a listener,

"A lot of the lads seem to be much happier nowadays."

"Yes, they are," he agreed. He was no more than twenty-eight in years, yet illness and suffering had given him a gray, aged look.

He reflected a moment and then said,

"Do you know what I've come to think? There's a harmony about life. When you put yourself in tune with that harmony, you sense a rightness about things. You know a peace in your heart."

"You've found that peace, then?"

"Yes, I reckon I have. I used to gripe and complain about everything—about the Nips, the Government, my buddies, myself."

"Most of us have been feeling that way," I acknowledged.

"Maybe we have. But I bet I was one of the worst."

"How do you figure the change came about?" I asked.

"It came gradually," he said. "I learned to accept things— to accept the Nips and their awfulness. I accepted my mates. I accepted myself. Then I stopped griping so much and tried to do what I could to help. Every little bit I gave made me seem more at ease with myself. I decided no matter what happens I've got to do what I believe to be right."

"And what do you mean by 'right'?"

He looked puzzled.

"I don't exactly know. It means—er—not thinking so much about yourself and—er—taking time to think about what you ought to do. I've never been much of a one to pray—but that's what I'm doing—I'm praying. Prayer makes me feel stronger, see—and then I'm ready for whatever is next."

"Is that what you meant by the harmony of life?"

"Yes, it is, I suppose. It's a power. When you get in line with it you know it and you know it's right."

"Isn't that the same thing as doing God's will?"

"I expect it is. I never went to service before."

"There were a lot like you," I said. "What seems to me important about a church is that we all come together as one when we open ourselves to God's will. You carry some of the harmony away with you when you leave the church."

He nodded, smiling. We shook hands and he left me.

Not many members of the Chungkai church were in this camp, but a few of us started services again in the open air. At one of the first of these services, a guard walked up to me while I was preaching and shouted,

"Curra, bagero!" He struck me on the face. I politely told him to go away. Strangely enough he did. Then he thought better of it, and came back to administer another slap before leaving us to finish the service in peace.

With us were three Church of England priests of strong Anglo-Catholic convictions. One of them was invited to give a series of addresses on the meaning of the Christian faith. He concentrated on the ceremonial aspect of worship. The first meeting was well attended. The second time his subject was the same. Fewer came. By the third meeting there was only a handful. It was obvious that the men wanted to go beyond ceremonials. They were more concerned with faith expressed through participation rather than with faith expressed through ritual and symbols.

Shortly after, a group voiced their desire for talks that would be more satisfying to the spiritual needs of the majority. Once more I found myself discoursing to an audience that grew steadily. Because this was a daily event I found it exhausting, but the interest and sympathy of my listeners kept me going.

In our nocturnal sessions by the bamboo grove at Chungkai we had grown to know Jesus. We had confined our explorations to a study of his life and teachings. Now, those of us who had moved on to Nakawm Paton were ready to proceed to an evaluation of what we had learned—both from our discussions and from our experience.

Some contemporary writers—Kafka, Sartre, Bennett, and Camus among them—have been credited with reminding theologians of the sinfulness of man. This was something of which we needed no reminder. We knew all about sin. We had seen for ourselves how low man could fall.

We wanted to learn what Christianity had to say about our redemption. Before we could do, we had to be. It was not only our minds but our wills that had to be changed. We had to be called into being by love. That lonely figure on the Cross had redeemed mankind by his love and sacrifice. Yet while that redemption was a once-for-all event, it is also a fact that we must be redeemed daily.

As guilty men we wanted to understand how the Christian life shared in the fate and condition of the world. Because we were men we could not escape our involvement in the world with all its imperfections. We were victims of the Japanese but we also shared their blood guilt. Like them, we had killed in battle and lived by the law of a life for a life, an eye for an eye, a tooth for a tooth, a hand for a hand, a wound for a wound, a stripe for a stripe.

We were involved because of our uncertainties. Not only our captors threatened us, but life itself. The props of Western civilization had been swept from under us and with them our faith in man and the things of man—his technology, his belief in progress, his utopianism, his rationalism, his pride. With others of the twentieth century, we hung suspended over the big hole, the abyss of meaninglessness, and the outlook was bleak.

We were involved, too, because of our doubts. Many of us had turned to Christianity from unbelief and still carried with us our fear of faith. We could say with Dostoevski: "It is not as a child that I believe and confess Jesus Christ. My 'hosanna' is born of a furnace of doubt."

Our doubts were our inheritance as children of our times.

We had two alternatives: we could choose the way of men, based on the sovereignty of the natural order, closed, sealed, and impersonal; or we could choose the way of Jesus Christ, free and personal, based upon the sovereignty of God, the Father.

The wind of the spirit had blown upon us; we could not prove how or whence it had come. But our experience pointed to a source beyond ourselves. We knew personal fulfillment, love, joy, peace, wholeness, as we committed ourselves to the One who called us. Only as we responded to this Word did we receive the power to progress toward true humanity.

Our life on the horizontal plane was made meaningful at the point where it was met by the vertical. At that point marked by the Cross we found ourselves.

It was almost time for Christmas. Our third year in captivity, the year 1944, was drawing to a close. But we were no nearer freedom than the year before. The only news we had came to us from our captors. They told us exuberantly that their armies had taken India and were about to join forces with Rommel in North Africa. Soon the war would be over and we could look forward to working for the Emperor in Japan. We knew this was not true. We were convinced that the war would end in our favor. But what interested us was, would we live long enough to see that end? How many more Christmases could we survive?

We were determined nevertheless to make Christmas a day to be remembered, like the last one. We planned a special church service and a program of recreation. A feature of the latter was to be a Derby, with the healthiest men as horses and the skinniest as jockeys. The cooks were preparing to tempt our palates with a holiday menu. We were working hard to get things ready, with each of us carrying out a special assignment, when a train pulled in on the siding. We saw bloody stretchers being lifted carefully out of the railroad cars.

We were summoned to help carry the wounded men to the operating hut. They had been brought here from the nearby camp of Nong Pladuk. From their lips we heard the story: While they were lining up for their evening ration, a squadron of our bombers had appeared without warning and dumped their load on the camp. Since Nong Pladuk was located beside a marshaling yard, our fliers had apparently mistaken it for a military base. One hundred and twenty-five men were killed outright and over four hundred injured.

The surgeons made ready to operate. The blood transfusion teams stood by. For the moment we forgot our Christmas plans in caring for the avalanche of wounded men. This development cast a pall over our spirits. But we were determined not to be overcome by it, and as soon as we were able, we resumed our preparations.

Christmas Day dawned warm, but not oppressive. Again I went early to church. But this time I was to be the preacher.

The hut was filling up. It was soon packed from wall to wall and overflowing through the doors. Before me were many nationalities—English, Welsh, Australians, Scots, New Zealanders, Americans, Dutch, Eurasians.

My heart swelled. Their faces were bearded, gaunt, hollow-cheeked, skin drawn tight over the bones. But determination was reflected in their eyes—and courage, faith, hope, and love. Gone was that empty look which revealed listlessness, fatalism, or despair. They had the air of men who would not be defeated whatever ordeals they faced.

Without benefit of instrumental accompaniment we all sang together with great gusto the traditional Christmas hymns. I spoke briefly, as Padre Webb had done last year, of the hope that Christmas brings. I pronounced the benediction and the men streamed out into the warm tropic sunlight.

Once more we had our Christmas dinner, topped off with the traditional Christmas pudding. This time the performance in the cookhouse impressed the Japanese. If these cooks could accomplish so much with so little, they reasoned, what couldn't they do if given a free hand? One of the officers decided to throw a party; he ordered the best cook to be sent to him for instructions.

The officer made it clear that he wanted a superfeast, Christmas style, for his guests. He told the chef that he was to spare no pains.

The dinner that night was the last word. The *pièce de resistance* was a work of art, a large bird shinily glazed and beautifully decorated. The chef described it as the kind of holiday turkey Americans ate at their family dinners. The Japanese guests gorged themselves, picking the bird to the bone.

That night a number of them became violently ill. The officer called the cook and demanded an explanation. In the Western world, the cook declared, the ceremonial fowl is viewed as a rich delicacy, to be eaten only in small quantities.

His answer seemed to satisfy the officer. Afterward we learned that the turkey was not a turkey at all, but a vulture. The cook had set a snare and caught it in the camp.

The year 1944 passed into 1945. Since we had no power for our radio, we learned nothing of how the war was going. Our only source of news was the Japanese, who delighted in telling us of their brilliant victories. But we did not believe a word they told us and remained firm in our belief that they would be defeated.

An Australian and an English chaplain reached the camp about this time. Between them they built up the church, and with it, the camp morale.

A growing nervousness gripped the Japanese. They ordered sudden roll calls in the middle of the night, making us tumble out, then keeping us standing on parade, often well into the next day. They raided our huts without warning, seizing any books or papers they could discover.

In one of these raids I lost my diary, my Greek grammar, and my Bible. I went to headquarters and demanded their return. The interpreter to whom I spoke refused to give back what I had written, although he did return my Bible, stamping his "chop," or identifying mark, on the flyleaf.

The Australian chaplain, Padre Hugh Cunningham, did not fare so well. The Japanese surprised him in the act of thumbing through a school atlas. They confined him in a bamboo cell so low he could not stand up in it, so narrow he could not sit down. To make doubly certain of his discomfort, a guard came by at intervals and prodded the padre with his bayonet.

Abruptly, our captors issued an order forbidding religious services, of which they were becoming increasingly suspicious. They had sworn to bring us to our knees; they had not done so. We had bent, but not broken. Out of a condition of no purpose had appeared men with purpose. If this improvement continued, the guards reasoned, our gatherings could become a potential nucleus for revolt. They also reinforced the ban against singing which they had relaxed after the completion of the bridge.

We had no intention of complying. On information passed from mouth to mouth, small knots of men assembled in different parts of the camp at irregular periods. Services were conducted somewhat in the manner of a Quaker meeting, with a lesson followed by questions and comment.

In some ways we were learning what it must have been like to be an early Christian. We had no building, no church headquarters, no permanent secretaries, no bishops, no moderators, no mimeographed directives; but the church kept living and growing. The Bible was keenly read and men kept praying. Prayer was essentially communion. We found that no matter where we were, what we were doing, or what was being done to us, we prayed. We prayed even as we were being beaten up by our captors.

After a while, in response to our petition, the authorities permitted us to resume our services. They stipulated, however, that a Japanese interpreter be present to make sure no one preached subversion.

Good Friday came. Regardless of denomination most of us decided to attend the Roman Catholic service at noon. We wanted to bow our heads and bend our knees before the Lord who had died for all of us.

In my contemplation, I recognized that it was no easy thing to call that figure on the cross "Lord." I heard his words: "Father, forgive them, for they know not what they do."

This he had said for his enemies. But what was I to say for mine? I could not say what he had said, for he was innocent whereas I was not. Humbly I had to ask, "Forgive me *and* mine enemies, for we know not what we do."

I said to myself,

"By his déath he gave to men the responsibility of caring for one another ánd doing his Father's will; to sons and mothers and fathers and brothers and sisters he assigned the task of caring for all other sons and mothers and fathers and brothers and sisters. No small commission.

"To call him 'Lord' meant there was no other way but his. Yet how could I follow him? I knew the Sermon on the Mount, but I lived by the laws and conventions of society—a society that condemned criminals to isolation or death, whereas he led them to Paradise.

"I called him 'Lord,' but with my fellow men worshiped Mammon in our temples of business. I had read that he was the Way, the Truth, and the Life. But we still clung to the belief that man was master of his fate, capable of building the equivalent of God's Kingdom through his own knowledge, his skills, and his technology.

"He asked us to believe in him. But it was much easier for us to believe in a president or dictator, a scientist, scholar, news commentator, movie actress, or baseball star. Any of these was more acceptable than a Jewish carpenter, condemned as a criminal, hanging on a bloody cross."

I confessed, "It is hard to be a disciple, Lord."

At dawn on Easter some of us slipped out of our huts to make our communion in the open at the edge of the camp. There we received the elements in token of our Lord's sacrifice, that we might be strengthened to follow "the Comrade-God who on the Cross was slain, to rise again."

When we finished, the sun was up. The darkness was still here, but it was being overcome by light. Death was here, but it was being redeemed by life, God's Life.

CHAPTER 10

The Last Trek

AGAIN WE RECEIVED ORDERS TO MOVE. WE WERE to be separated from the "other ranks" and confined to a camp for officers.

I learned that we were headed back to Kanburi, about sixty miles to the west of where we were now. This was familiar territory. Near Kanburi had been the marshaling base for supplies to build the bridge over the River Kwai. The camp was in full view of the bridge. Would we have to look at it every day, an unhappy reminder of those dark times when we were building it?

Old memories stirred.

As the train clacked along on its jungle track, my thoughts went back over the events of those long months. In perspective I could see what I had experienced was extraordinary—both at Chungkai, and later at Nakawm Paton.

At first both had been places of sickness and despair. Yet I had seen a Power at work to renew us. Men were still men, so I had seen selfishness. But I had also seen love. This love and the church without walls were related. The church, with all its imperfections, was the only visible earnest or guarantee of something greater. It set our feet on the way of an eternal pilgrimage and pointed us toward an unchanging goal—to the source of life and the City of God.

I recalled what Dostoevski had said in *The Possessed:*

"The one essential condition of human existence is that man should always be able to bow down before something infinitely great. If men are deprived of the infinitely great they will not go on living and will die of despair. The Infinite and the Eternal are as essential for man as the little planet on which he dwells."

I had seen that it was the response to the Infinitely Great which led men to greatness in themselves and to the transcending of their environment. It was not out of obedience to a system that men learned to serve one another. Rather, it was through faith—the faith that moved the will.

We had been at Kanburi only a few days when a guard informed us with glee that Franklin D. Roosevelt was dead and that Winston Churchill was seriously ill and not expected to live. The Allied war effort was therefore doomed to failure; an Axis victory was imminent.

To counter this propaganda we had the evidence of our senses. The sight of Allied bombers overhead was no longer a rare occurrence. They appeared in the sky every day, scorning the chatter of the ack-ack battery mounted near the bridge on the banks of the River Kwai.

One morning the sirens sounded. This time the planes came in low and pattern-bombed the bridge. At the edge of our camp a train was standing. From the air the train made the area appear to be a legitimate military target. The fliers then pattern-bombed Kanburi, killing about forty men.

The bombing continued for several days. Although damaged slightly, the bridge was not destroyed.

About a week later a thundering rumble announced the approach of another raid. At the sound of the motors our guards dived for the nearest and deepest place of shelter. From the high ground of the camp, not half a mile from the bridge, we had a grandstand view. We were able to enjoy the spectacle undisturbed.

The squadron was well-organized and thoroughly efficient in its task of destruction. As it zoomed overhead, two bombers detached themselves and swooped down on the ack-ack battery, silencing it on their first run. Now the formation broke up. Each plane, one at a time, made a run over the bridge. Against the blue skies the bombers were a pleasing picture as they circled to await their turns.

A plane passed and dropped its stick of bombs. A span of the bridge disappeared. Another plane and another dropped their loads. This went on until every span was removed. Each time bombs hit a span, the little crowd of emaciated men sitting on the hillside cheered wildly. They might have been applauding their favorite rugby team.

Except for the intermittent boom of the explosions and the roar of the engines, the mood was more like a holiday than an air raid.

We could see the river below us, the timbers collapsing into it as though overcome by weariness, while the bamboos on the banks sighed and shivered gently.

None of us had any love for that bridge. It had become a hated symbol—a symbol of Japanese power. Prisoners of war had been driven to build the bridge against their will. And as officers we had been forced at bayonet point to take part.

We watched the heavy beams floating in the river, and remembered how we had waded in with those timbers on our shoulders, fighting to keep from being swept away by the furious current. We remembered the makeshift pile driver and the impossible demands it made on our exhausted bodies as we lifted and dropped, lifted and dropped its heavy weight.

We remembered the determined attempts at sabotage: how we sawed the bolts half through when the attention of the guards could be diverted; how we unscrewed nuts that had been passed as "O.K." and smashed their threads.

We remembered one of our workmates with an imaginative

turn of mind, who had gathered queens of the white ant, a large jungle termite, and buried them beside the timbers in the hope they would eat away the supports.

The last span disappeared. A belly-based cheer went up from the hillside.

"Hey!" a voice beside me cried. "What if the Nips make us build it all over again?"

"Don't worry," said another P.O.W. consolingly. "They haven't the heart for it."

I could only hope that he was right.

Nothing remained of the bridge over the River Kwai but a mass of wreckage.

The bombers came over again to take a last admiring look at their handiwork. The pleasant sound of the engines died away into quiet. But not for long. Our guards, having crawled out of their hiding places, reacted from fear with shouts and curses and threats.

No other such incidents occurred to break the monotony. But the work load was not heavy and life might have been almost supportable except for the character of the camp commandant, who rightly belonged in a mental institution. He was a snarling misanthrope, a scowling, vicious sadist, ever on the lookout for trouble. He hated us, although we never knew why. But hate us he did, with a hatred that exuded from every pore. He went out of his way to create situations he could use as an excuse to torment us. He regularly baited prospective victims into making statements which he could interpret as a reflection on the Emperor.

On one occasion a British interpreter went to the assistance of an officer who was being tortured and recklessly protected him with his own body. Guards held the interpreter while the crazed commandant beat him with a heavy ruler. Still alive and bleeding profusely, the offender was thrown into a slit trench. The commandant ordered him kept there. Only a strong will enabled him to survive until his release.

It was hard to love such a man.

The tension in the camp increased. At almost any time of day or night the Japanese continued to spring their surprise raids. They kept us standing on parade while they searched our sleeping places. But now we had so little, there wasn't much they could find. Our razors had been taken from us and kept in a kiosk. We had to go there to shave. Many items, nevertheless, remained safely hidden: compasses, maps, knives, and a wireless set. One officer had a dachshund which he had kept with him all the way from Singapore. I concealed a roll of exposed film until I left Kanburi, when I buried it in a container along with the films of others. It was later retrieved.

The behavior of our guards was puzzling. Were they planning to massacre us? We had to face that possibility. If so, I decided to make my bid for freedom—even if it turned out to be no more than a bid.

I undertook a rigorous toughening-up program. I was already feeling better—aside from my periodic attacks of malaria—than at any time since my imprisonment. Every morning before reveille a friend and I did our exercises. We also volunteered for a team operating the hand pump that gave the Japanese their water supply. This puzzled our guards as it was hard work. But hard work was what we wanted.

The whole camp was to be moved, a few men at a time, to a new area northeast of Bangkok. Weary of Kanburi and its sour smells—for it was an old camp—I put in for one of the first parties to leave. Each consisted of about two hundred officers divided into three companies.

One of my responsibilities as section commander was the distribution of equipment that had been allotted to us to carry. Our gear included large, heavy dishes of awkward size, shovels, picks, and hammers.

The spiritual growth which I had been witnessing for the past year or so had mostly been manifest among the "other ranks." I had seen an attitude so well described by Lt. Gen. A. E. Percival in a letter written after the war:

Inspired by faith, the British soldiers in these camps displayed some of the finest qualities of their race. Courageous under repression and starvation, patient through the long years of waiting, cheerful and dignified in the face of adversity, they steadfastly resisted all efforts of the Japanese to break their spirit and finally conquered.

I had been impressed by those same qualities. I had faith in our Jocks. I had watched with pride their developing concern for one another. But not having had the same experience with my brother officers, I wasn't so sure about them. Had they, too, been touched by the love of God?

My doubts were soon dispelled. I was gratified to see how eagerly they accepted assignments, demonstrating their wish to do only what was best for all. Several of them came to me to volunteer for any distasteful chores.

Eastward we traveled through Banpong on toward Bangkok. Along the track we could see the damage done by the Allied Air Forces. Railway junctions and marshaling yards were in ruins. Often the train was switched to a temporary track, bypassing sections which had been destroyed. Occasionally we would wait while a train passed loaded with reinforcements bound for Burma. The troops looked woefully young. We saw a cavalry regiment ride by along the road. It had come all the way from China. Goodness knows how many months it had taken them to get this far. The ponies were scrawny; the leather in the reins and saddles was patched and broken.

Farther on, we were shoved off onto a siding for a lengthy stay. We found ourselves on the same track with several carloads of Japanese wounded. These unfortunates were on their own and without medical care.

No longer fit for action in Burma, they had been packed into railway cars which were being returned to Bangkok. They had been picked up and dropped off according to the makeup of trains. Whenever one of them died en route he was thrown off into the jungle. The ones who survived to reach Bangkok presumably would receive some kind of medical treatment. But they were given none on the way.

They were in a shocking state. I have never seen men filthier. Uniforms were encrusted with mud, blood, and excrement. Their wounds, sorely inflamed and full of pus, crawled with maggots. The maggots, however, in eating the putrefying flesh, probably prevented gangrene.

It was apparent why the Japanese were so cruel to their prisoners. If they didn't care a tinker's dam for their own, why should they care for us?

The wounded men looked at us forlornly as they sat with their heads resting against the carriages, waiting for death. They had been discarded as expendable, the refuse of war. These were the enemy. They were more cowed and defeated than we had ever been.

Without a word most of the officers in my section unbuckled their packs, took out part of their ration and a rag or two, and, with water canteens in their hands, went over to the Japanese train.

Our guards tried to prevent us, bawling, "No goodka! No goodka!" But we ignored them and knelt down by the enemy to give water and food, to clean and bind up their wounds. Grateful cries of "Aragatto!" ("Thank you!") followed us when we left.

An Allied officer from another section of the train had been taking it all in.

"What bloody fools you are!" he said to me.

"Have you never heard the story of the man who was going from Jerusalem to Jericho?" I asked him. He gave me a blank look, so I continued,

"He was attacked by thugs, stripped of everything, and left to die. Along came a priest who passed him by. Then came a lawyer, a man of high principles; he passed by as well. Next came a Samaritan, a half-caste, a heretic, an enemy. But he didn't pass by; he stopped. Kneeling down, he poured some wine through the unconscious man's lips, cleaned and dressed his wounds, then took him to an inn where he had him cared for at his own expense."

"But that's different!" the officer protested angrily. "That's in the Bible. These are the swine who have starved us and beaten us. These are our enemies."

"Who is mine enemy?" I demanded. "Isn't he my neighbor? God makes neighbors; we make enemies. That is where we excel. Mine enemy may be anyone who threatens my privileges—or my security—or my person—as well as those poor wretches who know no better. If they don't, we, at least, should. Whether we like it or not we are the ones who make the enemy and lose the neighbor. Mine enemy *is* my neighbor!"

He gave me a scornful glance and, turning his back, left me to my fulminations against society.

I regarded my comrades with wonder. Eighteen months ago they would have joined readily in the destruction of our captors had they fallen into their hands. Now these same officers were dressing the enemy's wounds.

We had experienced a moment of grace, there in those blood-stained railway cars. God had broken through the barriers of our prejudice and had given us the will to obey His command, "Thou shalt love."

The words of Jesus came to me:

"Ye have heard that it hath been said, Thou shalt love thy neighbor, and hate thine enemy. But I say unto you, Love your enemies, bless them that curse you, do good to them that hate

you, and pray for them which despitefully use you and perse-
cute you; that ye may be the children of your Father who is
in heaven."

The reply Reason had made to such a command was,

"But we have to be practical because we live in a practical
world. It doesn't pay to love—particularly your enemy."

Now Faith answered,

"Quite true. One need but to look at the Cross to see this
demonstrated. But—there is no other way to live. 'Except
a grain of wheat fall into the earth and die, it abideth by itself
alone.' "

Our experience of life in death had taught us that the way
to life leads through death. To see Jesus was to see in him
that love which is the very highest form of life, that love which
has sacrifice as the logical end of its action. To see this was
to see that the man who hoards up life's powers only to use
them for selfish purposes has but one end, that of death—
separation from God and others. What we hoard, we lose.
What we confine, we kill. To hang on to life, to guard it, to
preserve it, is to end up by burying it. Each of us must die to
the physical life of selfishness, the life controlled by our hates,
fears, lusts, and prejudices in order to live in the flesh the life
that is of the spirit. This is a basic law which cannot be broken
except at great cost.

We were beginning to see in this the purpose that transcends
all other purposes and makes them creative and meaningful.
We were beginning to understand that as there were no easy
ways for God, so there were no easy ways for us. God, we
saw, was honoring us by allowing us to share in His labors—
aye, in His agony—for the world He loves.

God, in finding us, had enabled us to find our brother.

A whistle blew. A train with a light load came along, picked
up our cars, and we were on our way. We found the bridge
over the River Tachin had been knocked out—not so thor-

oughly as the one over the Kwai—but thoroughly enough. Juggling our kit and tools, we shuffled across on a single plank high above the water.

Once on the other side, several of us were conscripted to load barges ferrying supplies across the river. It was hard coolie work performed under acute pressure and in scorching heat. I tried to take a drink of water; it made me froth at the mouth. A workmate gave me a pinch of salt and I was myself once more. The urgency with which the Japanese drove us had its cheering aspect—it could only mean reverses in Burma.

In Bangkok we were transferred from one railroad station to another. We marched along a picturesque canal. A highly decorated barge made a graceful picture as it cut through the reflection of the gilded Wat Arun pagoda.

Friendly Thais in their white suits and bright sarongs lined our path, shouting and cheering. They were trying to tell us something.

They held up their fingers in a V-for-Victory sign. We were familiar with the V-sign, but we had no idea what they were attempting to convey by it now. Did it express no more than partisan enthusiasm? Or did they have hopeful information? Mystified, but appreciating their gesture, I returned the salute. Suddenly the smiling faces disappeared in a rush of blackness. The next I knew I was lying on the ground, looking up at a guard standing ready to strike another blow. The indignant exclamations from the crowd, however, had their effect. After he had stormed at me a while, he lowered his rifle and allowed me to stagger to my feet. I considered the blow a fair price to pay for the friendship of the crowd.

We reached the other station where we were told there would be an all-day wait for the train.

Some P.O.W.'s were working in the yard. I recognized two of them as Argylls. Jumping up quickly, I ran to meet them.

But I was stopped short by a guard. Communication between different groups of prisoners was not tolerated.

I sat down in the shade of a warehouse close to the gang working under the watchful eye of a supervisor. Gradually I inched my way along without rising from a sitting position. After about an hour I reached the corner opposite the men. I gave a quick, low whistle. One of the Argylls glanced up, looked around, and was about to resume his work when he saw me sitting in the shadows.

"Come over toward me," I called in a loud whisper, "and we'll have a wee chat."

He nodded to show he had heard me. Then, keeping his back toward me, he pushed his hand truck in my direction. He threw a box on the ground. As he stooped to pick it up, he said,

"We'll have to be awfully careful. The Nips are keeping a tight guard on us."

"That's not a bad sign," I replied. "It must mean they've got the wind up. Do you have any news?"

He threw another box on the ground.

"Not even a rumor. We're a small camp—run by a Nip warrant officer. He's a regular bastard. We're always being beaten up and having our rations cut."

"Cheer up," I said. "As we passed through Bangkok, the Thais looked happy about something. I'm sure the news must be good. By the way, could you use any money?"

"Could I! Me and two other Argylls are mucking in together. One of them is pretty sick. The rest of us try to keep him going. If I could buy some food—"

"How can you buy food if the Nips won't let you speak to the Thais?"

"Nothing to it. We bribe the guards."

He glanced over his shoulder.

"The Pig has his eye on me. I'd better finish this load."

The guard was coming in his direction. He moved the hand-cart nearer the truck and lifted his last box. Picking up the handle of the empty cart, he passed near enough to whisper, "I'll be back."

The "Pig" was now quite close and stood berating him. He was facing the sun so he couldn't see me in the shadows. I sat there without moving, waiting for the Argyll to come back. After a long ten minutes he returned, pulling an enormous stack of boxes.

"You'd think I was a bloody donkey, wouldn't you?" He brought the cart to a stop. Then he said, "You'd better hop it or they'll beat the life out of you."

"Dinna worry," I replied. "They'll not do that."

I fumbled at my waist. I had over fifty bahts of my pay tucked into my kilt.

"I'm putting this money under a stone. When you've finished pick it up."

I held up the stone for him to see.

"Best of luck. Give my love to the boys."

"That I'll do. And thanks for the cash."

"Good-by. God bless you."

"Good-by, sir. And God bless you."

Under the watchful eye of the "Pig" he resumed loading more energetically than before, while I inched my way back along the shadows to rejoin my party.

It was well after dark when the train came. We rode all night standing up. We were dumped out at dawn by a roadside and ordered to march. We found ourselves in the midst of paddy fields stretching away into nowhere.

We began to march. As the sun climbed, the heat became stifling, for it was about the hottest time of the year. At noon we were halted briefly and allowed to boil some water to drink. There was almost nothing left to eat, since our journey had taken longer than expected.

On the road again. A big car drove up. A Japanese officer glared at us, glanced at his watch, told our guards to hurry us up, then drove away. The heat grew so intense that the metal of our tools and utensils blistered our fingers at the touch. Again we had no water and no salt. The afternoon seemed unending.

With the coming of night the temperature dropped; it seemed chilly by contrast. Then the rain started to pour with all the sudden ferocity of the tropics. The road was a quagmire. The whole countryside was a swamp. Our packs took on the weight of lead. At every step the suction of the mud dragged us down. Some faltered and could not go on. Their burdens were shouldered by others. With our arms around the flagging, we made it into Camp Nakon Nyok at about four in the morning. It had taken us almost twenty-four hours to march the forty miles.

We were assigned space in a half-completed hut and fell asleep as we were, caked with mud. At six I was awakened with a shake and ordered to produce four officers for a work party at once. I thought this was unfair and said so bluntly. But no one paid attention.

Taking note of our surroundings, we found we were right in the middle of a military position the Japanese were preparing for their defense. It was apparently intended to block an invasion following a possible Allied landing on the coast near Bangkok. We were at the base of the foothills. Between us and the shore there was nothing but a great flat plain of paddy fields. Troops came and went. We could hear big guns being moved into place. On a steep hill above us, we could see an observation post being constructed. Here the Japanese were making ready for a last desperate stand.

We had to admit our prospects did not look bright. Japanese officers scowled at us as they rode by on horseback. The air crackled. The camp commandant, the same one we'd had at Kanburi, appeared and was immediately more demanding and nastier than ever.

Every day there was a cluster of prisoners staked to the ground in front of the guardhouse. We had no news of the war's progress, but we could feel the Japanese were worried.

One morning we had gone to work as usual. This time we were to carry rocks down the hill to ballast the road we were building.

About mid-morning our guards disappeared. We took advantage of their absence by lying down to rest. After several hours they returned drunk. They motioned us to pack up and go back to camp.

"This is it!" I said excitedly to Blondie, a friend of mine, as we started back to camp.

"What do you mean?"

"The Japs are licked. The show is over. They've thrown in the sponge."

My companion was more conservative.

"Take it easy, don't get your hopes up," he said. "Tell me what have you got to go on?"

We were marching past the guardhouse. The ground in front of it was empty.

"What do you make of that, Blondie? Where do you suppose the poor blighters are who were staked out there this morning?"

He refused to be impressed.

"Oh, I dunno. Perhaps they've been released."

"You can bet they've been released. Tell me—when do you remember seeing that piece of ground free of prisoners?"

He couldn't say.

"And they're not the only ones who'll be released. Wait and see."

"Oh, I dunno," he said. "I dunno about that."

About the middle of the evening news spread through the

camp that the Japanese commandant had sent for Lt. Col. Toosey, the British senior officer.

I was sitting in our hut with John Leckie and several of my other friends, wondering what was happening. We hadn't long to wait for an answer. Word flashed from one end of the camp to the other. In the dim light of the palm-oil lamp faces shone. Silently we shook hands.

Someone started singing. Then everyone was singing with one powerful voice. The song was quickly taken up; it resounded from hut to hut. From everywhere it came—Elgar's *Pomp and Circumstance*:

> *"Land of hope and glory*
> *Mother of the free*
> *How shall we extoll Thee*
> *Who are born of Thee?*
> *Wider still and wider*
> *Shall thy bounds be set*
> *God who made thee mighty*
> *Make thee mightier yet."*

Next we sang "God Save the King." After that we sang "Jerusalem the Golden" and "The Twenty-third Psalm." We sang and kept on singing. It was hearty singing—the singing of free men.

We noticed that our guards had vanished. They had melted into the night. There was a reason for this. The Japanese military had been accustomed to singing war chants to prepare themselves for battle. When they heard our hearty singing, they concluded we were planning to slaughter them, so they took to the hills.

It was late before the camp returned to silence.

Before reveille I was outside the hut, doing my exercises, bending and stretching, bending and stretching, when I sensed I was being watched. Turning around, I saw a guard standing at attention about ten yards away. When he noticed me, he bowed and kept on bowing. I thought he must be trying to imitate me. But his bows weren't deep enough for that.

Not knowing what else to do, I smiled at him. He smiled back.

"Okayga?"

"Okayga."

Without waiting for further word he streaked for the hills. Presumably he had been sent to see what we were up to.

The Japanese returned to their quarters one or two at a time, keeping their distance. Though we held the power, it never occurred to us to raise a hand against them.

The moment of grace by the railway siding was no temporary experience. This same situation held true in other camps. The incoming liberators were so infuriated by what they saw that they wanted to shoot the Japanese guards on the spot. Only the intervention of the victims prevented them. Captors were spared by their captives. "Not an eye for an eye, a limb for a limb this time," said these exhausted but forgiving men.

Like faith and forgiveness, freedom isn't something talked about. It has to be enacted.

After breakfast John Leckie and I simultaneously felt that on this, our first morning of freedom, we had to climb that hill behind the camp. While we made our way to the top we saw others who had the same impulse. There were scattered groups of men, some ahead of us, some behind us, going up in silence.

We reached the top. Stretching out before us, as far as we could see, was the brown and green patchwork quilt of the paddy fields.

We stood in quiet reverence, gazing out over those fields to the horizon, toward Chungkai where our friends had died.

We spoke the words of the 121st Psalm: "I will lift up mine eyes unto the hills."

Freedom burst out all over.

When the Japanese commandants had read the order granting P.O.W.'s permission to fly their flags and to play national anthems, they were only carrying out a formality. They did not expect these things to happen.

At a nearby camp, however, within minutes of the reading of the order, an enormous Union Jack was flying bravely from the flagpole. That banner had been carried through the death camps of the railroad for this moment—by an Argyll who never doubted the day of victory would come. The Japanese had not discovered it. He had made his blanket into a sleeping bag with the Union Jack inside.

At our own camp a flag was found and hoisted. As we looked at it waving proudly, we saw it as a symbol of our liberty—our liberty founded upon the Cross; for the Union Jack is composed of three crosses, the Cross of St. George, the Cross of St. Patrick, and the Cross of St. Andrew.

Soon afterward a fellow Argyll, David Boyle, had the pleasure of going to the Japanese commandant and demanding a battery to operate our wireless. The commandant stared at him.

"Battery? Wireless? But you can't have a wireless!"

"We've had one here for quite a while," David informed him.

"But how? How did you get it in?"

"*You* brought it in for us."

"No. I wouldn't do that."

"You did, though. You brought it in from Kanburi—with that loot you had in your baggage."

The commandant was speechless.

David went on,

"We knew your searches were so thorough that we didn't have a chance in hell of smuggling the wireless into camp unless we sent it in with *you*."

"But—but—" The commandant was still nonplussed. David spelled it out for him.

"Remember the squad you detailed to load your baggage for you? They slipped the set in . . . Another squad slipped it out again after you got here . . . Now, how about the battery?"

"Certainly, certainly," said the commandant, coming to attention and bowing. "You shall have it right away."

As David started to leave, the commandant said hastily,

"There are no hard feelings, I hope. If my actions have seemed unkind, it was not my intention. I was only acting according to orders. I like you all."

"Quite," David said. He turned his back on the commandant and walked out.

(The list of the commandant's crimes was so long that eventually he was sentenced by his own superiors to life imprisonment. Soon after that he was tried again by the Allied Tribunal and received the death sentence.)

We put our wireless into operation at once. We learned then that Russia had declared war on Japan, and that the atom bombs had been dropped. But we also learned of the Japanese directive ordering that if Admiral Mountbatten landed troops in Thailand, all officers in prison camps were to be killed. At the same time we heard that our new camp had been observed and was presumed to be for Japanese troops. Therefore it was scheduled to be bombed by the R.A.F. The Mountbatten landings were set for August 28, the R.A.F. bombings for August 17. Since the day of liberation was August 16, our margin of safety was not very great. Had the war continued for two more weeks, we would have "copped it" one way or another, at the hands of friend or foe.

We stayed on in camp while we waited for our orders. The Japanese quartermasters released Red Cross parcels to us. Our faces fell when we saw they were marked "September, 1942." We found their contents completely unusable.

Whatever entertainment there might be we had to provide for ourselves, but we were old hands at it by now. Willing workers quickly erected a stage on which was produced a Liberty Review, including a Victory Can-Can danced and sung by a chorus of "the short and the fat and the tall." Ponies were confiscated from a Japanese cavalry unit for a genuine Liberty Derby.

Our first visitor from the outside world was an American paratrooper from the Midwest who had lost his way and wandered into our camp. We wondered what he must have thought as he was seized by a yelling crowd of skinny, bronzed, bearded, half-naked savages who bore him on their shoulders through the camp.

We carried him to our makeshift stage and kept him there for hours, bombarding him with queries, while he recounted, blow by blow, the entire course of the war, regaling us with everything that happened during our three and a half years of silence. To us he was the living embodiment of the freedom we had dreamed of and longed for all that time.

Communications of a sort were soon established. Oxcarts bumped and lurched over the muddy roads, since no other vehicles could get through. They brought us food, medicines, and decent clothing and eventually the first mail from home in nearly four years.

This time I was among the lucky ones. When the G's were called, there was a packet of blue envelopes addressed in my father's characteristically bold handwriting—just as I had seen them in my dreams many months before. For the first time I learned of what had been happening at home.

But joy was mingled with sadness. An officer next me went through his mail, looking for a letter from his wife. There was none. He opened another letter—one from a friend—and learned that his wife had died.

But there was something we craved even more than mail—news of our missing comrades. So many had gone off up-country on some work party, and we had never seen them since. We wanted to know where they were, how they had fared —above all, if they were still alive. The men in the ration parties became our unofficial network of information. They made it their business to pick up all the personal news they could glean at one camp and pass it on to the next. Before the oxcart had come to a stop they would find themselves surrounded with anxious questioners.

"Have ye heard anything of my mucker? Name of Mac-Intosh. He was a sergeant in the Field Artillery—the Hundred Twenty-second. About middle-sized, he was. With dark brown hair. Expect he'd be wearing a beard."

Usually the couriers shook their heads. Once in a while a name would give them a clue. Now and then the news was good; more often it was not. Death was continuing to take its toll. For many deliverance had been in sight. But, like Moses, they had died before they could enter the Promised Land.

The name uppermost in my mind was Dusty Miller's. Whenever an oxcart appeared, I was in the front rank of questioners.

I was looking forward to a reunion with Dusty and Dinty Moore. At every opportunity I asked visitors from other camps if they had any word. Time and again I put the same question and gave the descriptions. Repeatedly, I received the same reply,

"Sorry, chum, I don't remember anyone by that name—or who fits the way you describe him. Could you give me a clue?"

It was from one of the couriers that I learned how Dinty Moore had died. But there was still no word of Dusty. Then at last I met a courier who had been on the same work detail with him.

"Yes, I knew him," he said. "We were sent to Burma to cut a retreat route for the Japs. He was one of those left behind after the road was built to maintain it during the monsoon."

"Where is he now?" I asked.

The man was reluctant to speak. He stammered for a minute or two. Then he replied,

"We had a pretty bad time of it. It was a repeat performance of the railroad. And those who were left behind had an even harder time—especially after the Japs knew they were going to lose.

He stopped.

"But what about Miller?" I asked again.

The man looked away.

"The last news I had of him wasn't good."

"What was it then?"

"According to what I heard, he was in trouble."

"Dusty?"

"He got the Nip warrant officer in charge of his party down on him."

"What had he done wrong?"

"That was it. He hadn't done anything wrong." He swallowed hard. "The Nip hated him because he couldn't break him. You know how he was—a good man if ever there was one. That's why he hated him."

"What did the Nip do to him?"

"He strung him up to a tree."

I was aghast.

"You mean—"

Then came the simple reply,

"Yes. He crucified him."

I could hardly speak.

"When?"

"About the beginning of August."

"Just before the Japs—"

"—packed up, yes."

He turned away. He had said as much as he could bear.

I was so stunned I didn't quite know what to do. I walked out from the group of chattering questioners.

Dusty dead?

Dusty—the man of deep faith and the warm heart—the man who was incapable of a mean act, even against a brutal tormentor. He had been rewarded for his goodness by hatred —his radiant goodness which must have maddened the warrant officer to the point where he went berserk.

There, like his Master, he died, so far from his homeland, so far from everyone, yet so near to God.

I moved off to a corner of the camp that I might bear my grief alone. The surroundings misted so that nothing was clear any more; there was only the reality of suffering, disappointment, and sorrow.

Then I could see once again the light that had challenged the darkness in the valley of the shadow—the light that had been reflected from gentle faces.

I could see Ian Carruthers reliving his boyhood and remembering the yachts that sailed on the Clyde.

I could see Dodger Green talking eagerly and wistfully to me as he groped for the truth he was beginning to apprehend.

I could see Dinty Moore restoring my spirits with his quick wit and kindly humor as he performed some menial task.

I could see Dusty Miller kneeling before me with his rag and his basin, telling me with a smile of his plans for the future as he cleaned my ulcers.

I could see the young lad dying while I held his hand, and saying,

"It's all right. I'm glad it's all right."

The words of St. Paul came to me:

"For God, who commanded the light to shine out of darkness, hath shined in our hearts."

It was that light which I had seen in so many faces that helped me to see in my own darkness.

CHAPTER 11

Through the Valley

WHEN WE THOUGHT OF RETURNING HOME WE saw ourselves as ghosts of the past. The Britain most of us had known was the Britain of 1939. Six years had gone by; and six years is a long time when one is in his twenties. Our friends and families would have changed as well as we. They had known us as boys; we were going back as war-hardened men.

On a night of hammering rain the order came: "Pack up! You're on your way to Bangkok!" We began the last lap out as we had ended the last lap in, slogging it on foot through that heavy, squelchy mud. But trucks were waiting for us at the road end—trucks with respectful Japanese at the wheel. On our way across Bangkok to the airfield we went by the spot where the guard had struck me with his gun butt for holding up my fingers in the V-sign. It had happened only a short while ago; yet the event seemed of another time.

While we waited in the hangar for our plane to come, we saw our first white woman in three and a half years, a blonde, shapely Norwegian. She had been interned with her husband and had come to feed the former P.O.W.'s. She was beautiful. The sight of her reminded us that there were other places and other ways of living and that we were on our way to them.

The Japanese had given us the backlog of pay due us for

three and a half years. It was in bahts which had dropped so greatly in value that when four of us who were traveling together pooled our resources, we had no more than enough to buy a fruit salad. We argued over the amount of vitamins in that salad but agreed it was tastier by far than the vitamin pills we were now being given in huge quantities to swallow daily.

Next morning we boarded a Dakota and took off to the west for Rangoon. Our pilot had heard that I had been a flier at one time. He kindly invited me to be co-pilot.

I looked down, following closely the trail of the railroad etched through the jungle along the valley of the Kwai. The pilot was watching me.

"I'll bet you're glad to be away from all that," he said.

"Too right I am!"

"We heard now and then how you were being treated," he continued sympathetically. "Native agents smuggled word through to Intelligence. Must have been tough."

"Yes, it was tough, all right."

The pilot handed me a packet of K-rations.

"Here, have something to chew on until we land at Rangoon."

The K-rations tasted like manna from heaven, so much so, in fact, that I concluded the present-day soldier was being spoiled. Then I laughed at myself. Already I was an old soldier, disapproving of the new.

We flew past the vacancy that now marked the spot where we had built the bridge over the River Kwai. We flew on, past Chungkai, Tonchan, Kinsao, Takanun—places we had known so well, places where so many of our friends had died. The flight, which otherwise was like an outing, was saddened by memories.

Not only had we come through the valley, we were above

it. We were on the high road home—a road that had taken
me six years to find. I recalled the words of the old Scot's
song:

> *"For ye'll tak' the high road and I'll tak' the low road*
> *And I'll be in Scotland afore ye*
> *For me and my true love will never meet again*
> *On the bonnie, bonnie banks of Loch Lomond."*

According to what I had been told as a child, this was a
message sent by a highland chieftain to his beloved before
his execution in Carlisle during Prince Charlie's retreat from
the attainment of his hopes and of his kingdom. The low
road was the way of death—the way so many of my friends
had taken.

A poignant recollection stirred in my mind. I had been
wounded in the right shoulder in Malaya and sent back to
Singapore to recover. Before I was released to rejoin the
remnant of the battalion I learned that my friend Gordon
Shiach had been badly hurt and was in another hospital. I had
known Gordon when we were schoolboys. We had been on
a cruise for Scottish secondary schools in the Baltic. I hadn't
seen him again until the day I left Stirling Castle as he was
entering with a squad of recent recruits. Eventually he had
been posted to us in Singapore.

While the battalion was in action in Malaya, he had been
returning from brigade headquarters with a supply of maps
when he was attacked by an enemy tank. Although desperately
wounded in the stomach, he had continued to drive his
wreck of a car back to the battalion.

As soon as I saw him I knew the end was not far off. His
brown eyes stared at me as I entered the ward. He recognized
me. He smiled when I greeted him, and said,

"I'm glad you've come. You're a breath of home."

It would have been pointless to bring him any delicacies

since he could not eat, so I had bought a little book containing excerpts of prose and poetry about Scotland. I said,

"There, that will give you a picture of what things are like."

Thumbing through the book, he stopped.

"Yes, that's home all right."

He looked up and handed me back the book open at the "Canadian Boat Song."

While I read I could see home through Gordon's eyes. There was the wide Firth stretching out before me as I stood on one of the Cowal hills that watched over it. On the silver-blue, ever-changing waters were the white wings of yachts bearing their happy crews along on pleasant cruises. The Sleeping Warrior of Arran and the hills of the Atlantic coastline formed a velvet picture frame for the homeland we knew so well.

> *"Listen to me as when of old our father*
> *Sang songs of other shores*
> *Listen to me and then in chorus gather*
> *All your deep voices as you pull your oars*
> *Fair these broad meads, these hoary woods are grand*
> *But we are exiles from our native land*
> *From the lone shielding of the misty island*
> *Mountains divide us, and the waste of seas—*
> *Yet still the blood is strong, the heart is Highland*
> *As we in dreams behold the Hebrides."*

That poem is the heart's cry of the exile.

A dark shadow stirred in the corner of the ward. The summer breeze of the Scottish hills was displaced by the sticky heat of Singapore. Both of us felt the same sharp thrust of homesickness.

Like Gordon, men had their dream of home. They had fought for it on the battlefield; it had sustained them in the prison camp. So many would never see home again.

Those of us who had survived were going there now.

Others would follow, flying above the River Kwai. This brought to mind the words of Isaiah:

"And an highway shall be there, and a way, and it shall be called The way of holiness; . . . the wayfaring men, though fools, shall not err therein."

We were far up along the Kwai, nearing the Three Pagodas Pass. A storm struck. The Pass was wreathed in a veil of swirling clouds and ghostlike shadows.

Then for a moment the clouds parted. There was a burst of sunlight. Far below we could see the end of the valley.

It looked so small.

The clouds closed in again. We continued on our way.

. . . and After

THE DAKOTA CIRCLED OVER RANGOON TO GIVE US OUR
first view of the city and the first glimpse of our Army in occupation. Tree-fringed lakes and the Great Pagoda contributed to the
air of peace and serenity.

We landed and were immediately escorted to a huge marquee
staffed by members of the Women's Volunteer Service from Great
Britain. The tent was filled with card tables set for tea; smiling
English ladies in light tropical dresses were in attendance. It is
hard to describe the exquisite taste of the freshly-made white bread
sandwiches and freshly-brewed tea. We were able to taste and see
things in a new way and to enjoy them more than we ever had
before.

I was savoring my sixth cup when I looked up to see four men
waiting near me as one of the ladies came to their table with tea.
They had tears in their eyes and their adam's apples were working
overtime. These men were tough, tougher than most. They had
proved they could stand up to beatings and torture. But to be
served with kindness had moved them so deeply that they stood
silently, in great humility. There was a spiritual beauty about those
four sun-blackened, bearded men as they stood, barefoot and
ragged, trying to hide their emotions.

We checked in at the military hospital set up in the dormitories
and buildings of Rangoon University by Lake Victoria. Our rags
were taken from us and burned. We were given green jungle shirts
and trousers, soap and towel, toothbrush and toothpaste. I watched
my blanket being tossed on the fire. When it was held up I

could see daylight through it. In the center was a huge round patch of orange canvas which made it look like a darkened Japanese flag.

We could hardly eat supper. The tea had been more than sufficient for our needs. That night as I tucked myself into a real bed with real sheets, I sighed in contentment.

Next morning when one of the nursing sisters entered the ward, she said, "I've never had patients like these in all my nursing experience. Everyone has made his own bed and men are competing for the privilege of sweeping the wards." This expressed the attitude of these P.O.W.'s. They lived not to be served but to serve.

At the end of October we embarked on a Dutch ship for Blighty. Our feelings were mixed as we waved farewell to Rangoon, the East, and our years of captivity. The jungle had been challenging, there had been comradeship of the highest order, and we had found a way of life that proved to be vital, meaningful, and beautifully sane. By the deaths of so many of our friends we were tied to those places with invisible cords that could never be broken.

I was musing by the rail when I noticed John Leckie standing next to me.

"Well," he said, "it's all over. I wouldn't have missed it for anything. True, it was rough. But I learned an awful lot that I couldn't have learned at university or anywhere else. For one, I've learned about the things of life that are real and for another, I've learned it's great to be alive."

It was easy for me to see how he could make such a remark. The experiences we had passed through deepened our understanding of life and of each other. We had looked into the heart of the Eternal and found Him to be wonderfully kind.

We made our first contact with the world we had left behind us as we were steaming up the Mersey to our berth in Liverpool. Word went around the ship that the longshoremen were about to strike for higher wages. They agreed, however, to handle our ship before they did so.

Our Jocks were worried that people on shore would not get their rations if ships were not permitted to dock. A delegation came to see me.

"Couldn't we work the docks?" their spokesman asked. "After all, we've done it before and we can do it again."

I promised I'd do what I could. As soon as we landed I went to a harbor master. He heard me out, all the while looking at me as though I were daft. Then he informed me that to accept the Jocks' proposal would precipitate a national crisis. The labor unions would oppose it; the Army would forbid it.

We thought we had come home to freedom. While we were prisoners we had been free to contribute to the general good, to create order out of disorder. Here, in a society which paid lip service to freedom, we were prohibited, apparently, from applying the lessons we had learned. Impersonal laws, red tape, regulations in triplicate, were hemming us in like the jungle with invisible walls.

This harsh impression, however, was mellowed by the warm welcome accorded by friendly citizens who shouted, shook our hands, and thrust bottles of beer upon us as our lorries drove through the streets of Liverpool.

An express train took us to Glasgow. My brother was waiting at the station barrier. I went with him to the hotel to cancel the reservation he had made in my name, as I had arrived in time to get home for the night.

I thought I was looking fairly respectable in my battle jacket and kilt, war-stained though it was. But the hall porter thought otherwise. He told me that filthy luggage such as mine could not be left in the hall. I glanced down at my gear. My belongings—a mud-stained green army pack and a kit bag—looked decent enough to me.

I picked up the offending items to take them away before some civilian had his sensibilities affronted by a dab or two of blood and mud.

The day of the soldier was over.

A November moon shone brightly over the hills in the early hours of the morning, its face reflected on the surface of the Firth of Clyde, as I saw the familiar shape of the home where I had said "Good-by, Mother," "Good-by, Dad" six long years ago.

Lights burned in the windows. My parents were waiting up to welcome me. This meeting was the greatest shock of all. Time had not dealt kindly with them. The years of uncertainties and fears, of waiting, hoping, and praying, had taken their toll. I had left them in summer; I had returned in winter.

Home again. But for what and to do what?

First we had to cope with the exasperating, bewildering mechanics of readjustment. Each experience brought its rude revelation.

I was luckier than most, for I was helped through mine by the sympathy and understanding of a girl whom I had known since my youth, Helen McIntosh Robertson of Sandbank in the Holy Loch. Helen met me on my return. She was courageous enough to marry me seventeen days later.

The frictions of adjusting to civilian life began almost at once. On the day before I was to be "demobbed," I came down with one of my recurrent attacks of malaria. I was shivering as I passed through the demobilization center. I suggested that perhaps my discharge ought to be deferred until I had proper medical treatment. This put sand in the well-oiled machinery, and, in fact, made it stagger to a standstill. The medical officer told me firmly that nothing could be done. Once on the conveyor belt, I had to stay there until discharged at the other end in a "civvie" suit.

When I grew stubborn about it, someone pressed the panic button. A solemn-looking individual appeared and questioned me with the professional patience of one accustomed to dealing with difficult children or imbeciles. He then asked me what I thought was wrong.

"Malaria!" I retorted. "That's what's wrong!"

"M-hmm," he said, as though disposing of that irrelevancy. Then, fixing me with a standard smile, he asked,

"Is there something worrying you, or are you afraid of anything?"

"Yes, I am very much afraid that I am going to have malaria at my own expense—whereas I would rather have it at the Army's."

"Quite understandable, quite, quite," he said, nodding sagely. Then, to humor me, he added, "Now that you're home, you know, you have absolutely nothing to worry about—nothing at all, whatever."

Conscious that I was up against an immovable object, I smiled as sweetly as I could and inquired,

"How do you know?" Then I added abruptly, "Never mind. I've had no medical treatment in the last three and a half years. I expect I can do without it now."

I stepped back into line; the machine shuddered into action, and I emerged with my gray flannel suit. It was too short and too wide.

A few weeks later I was admitted as a civilian to a hospital for tropical diseases, suffering not only from malaria, but from avitaminosis, hepatitis, enlarged heart, and ulcerated intestines from harboring overfriendly amoebae. It took eight weeks to straighten me out, but I was to follow a restricted program for the next two years. This included swigs of hydrochloric acid with every meal, for the acid buds of my stomach had been destroyed.

I was faced with a clothing problem; all I had to put on my back was the one ill-fitting suit. When I went around to the stores I learned no suits were available because of rationing. Then I was told with a sly wink that if I produced someone who could grant a favor for a favor a transaction might be arranged. I found everything was done on this basis.

When it came to choosing our lifework, we found many forces operating to frustrate our enthusiasms. We had been sent as boys to do men's work on the battlefield. Now that we returned as men we were offered boys' work.

Counselors with gray hair admonished us from behind their desks that we could now begin to live the British way by "joining the team," "toeing the party line," and "getting on the ball." Concerning affairs of state, wiser heads than ours would guide us. The inference was that now we were out of prison camp, we could put God away until Sunday. And with Him, our neighbor.

We weren't easy to live with. We were tense and taut. Not for long could we remain doing nothing. Rather than sit in a chair we would pace the floor; rather than stay at home we would go out and walk for miles. Sleep was of short duration. As soon as we awoke we'd be on the prowl again, looking for something to do or someone to meet.

We had enormous reserves of nervous energy to be used. Ideas popped up in our minds with amazing rapidity. Convinced that every one of them was good, we would rush from one place to another, trying to put them into action. Brazenly, we told our political friends how the country should be governed; we told our friends in the school system what they ought to do to improve education; we told our friends in the clergy how to bring their churches up to date.

It is not surprising that we were moody, restless, and irritable. We felt that at any moment we might be seized and deprived of our freedom. The Japanese were still with us; they entered our dreams. If we dreamed of the day's events in our new environment, the guards would be there, walking unnoticed among the people in the street. If we strolled past with a friend, they'd reach out and grab us. We'd cry out as they dragged us off to a punishment cell. But no one would come to our aid and there was no escape.

If we dreamed of open fields or rolling moors, our old hosts would be there, advancing, closing in on us from every side. No matter how hard we tried to flee, they would always catch us.

These dreams dogged us for years. One never knew when they would recur. I had such an experience many months after my return, when, in the course of my theological studies, I had gone to the United States to pursue postgraduate work in history at Hartford Theological Seminary in Hartford, Connecticut.

One day I was traveling by train from Hartford to New York and I fell asleep. As the train pulled into New Haven I was jolted suddenly awake. When I opened my eyes it was not New Haven that I saw, but a railroad stop in the jungle. The carriage was a boxcar type without seats or windows. My fellow passengers were all P.O.W.'s. The uniformed men on the platform were armed Japanese guards. It was only with the cry of "Sandwiches, ice cream, and candy" that the scene faded and New Haven became New Haven again.

We hungered for one another's company and for the comradeship we had shared. Our friends probably had the impression that our imprisonment was one huge, rollicking party. We fought off a great loneliness—a loneliness felt most keenly by those who worked with civilians that had never known the uncertainties of the front line or of prison camps. Our loneliness was increased by the fact that so many of our friends had not returned. Old familiar spots were haunted with their faces.

Whenever we met with other former P.O.W.'s, we loved to talk of the brilliant plans we'd made and the great things we were going to do. We were convinced that we had learned lessons important to mankind and we were eager to implement them.

We thought we had come home to a world at peace; instead we found a world preparing for the next war. Having had as much reason to hate as anyone, we had overcome hatred. Yet we came back to a world divided by hatreds. Communist hated capitalist; capitalist hated communist; Arab hated Jew; Jew hated Arab; labor hated management; management hated labor; politician hated politician.

A moral cynicism was sapping the strength of society. Half-lies were not only condoned, but regarded as smart. There were many who had remained untouched by the welter of the holocaust. What had happened on the battlefields, in mass bombings, in concentration camps—the blood, pain, suffering, heartbreak, and death—remained totally beyond their comprehension.

They did not share in the hopes and agony of mankind; they had no sympathy, no sense of involvement; they had no part in the universal fellowship of those who bear the mark of pain. Ever so brightly and ever so meanly they prostrated themselves before the Almighty Dollar and the Trembling Pound. We encountered those who were actually sorry to see the war end because they had had such a good time and done so well financially. Nations had survived this war; but few people asked, "For what?"

The men with dry souls said, "Let us go back to the good old days." They wanted to draw the blinds on everything that had happened in between. There were no lessons to be learned, no decisions made, no risks taken, no new pilgrimages started, no adventures in partnership with God begun.

Everyone spoke of seeking security. But what did security mean, but animal comfort, anesthetized souls, closed minds, and cold hearts?

It meant a return to the cacophonous cocktail party as a substitute for fellowship, where, with glass in hand, men would touch each other but never meet. They would speak, but nothing would be said and nothing heard. They would look at their partners, but would not see them. With glassy eyes they would stare past them into nothingness.

It meant a return to the cheap love made possible by contraceptives whereby male and female used each other as a thing, taking their share of sex in the same way they took their cocktails and wondering where was the fulfillment, where was the satisfaction. With the despairing cry of "I must be loved!" they would return periodically from the psychiatrist's couch to seek new partners and new problems. All the while their ears remained closed to the divine imperative, *"Thou shalt love!"*

It meant a return to the sedative at night and the stimulant in the morning; drugged sleep dulled the pain of existence and perked-up glands helped face the fears of the day.

It meant a return to the faceless mass; to culture dragged down to the level of advertising media; to education, not as an instrument for enrichment and enlightenment but as a tool for mass conditioning.

It meant a return to faith in technology and the Big Machine. As their powers were used to unleash yet greater hidden forces in nature, so men would find themselves more than ever enslaved and ever more ready to use those forces to bring about the total destruction of humanity. The contributions of free men seeking to serve the Infinitely Great in honesty, responsibility, and love would be denied. Socrates would have to drink his cup of hemlock again, the prophets be stoned. New Hitlers, new Mussolinis, would emerge. Atheistic materialism would fetter men to a hard, knobbly universe in which humanity was rejected.

In short, it meant flight from God and descent into the hell of loneliness and despair.

And where, in all this, was the vision of the Infinitely Great? Where was the place for those who wished to follow that vision, inspired, sustained, and uplifted by it to find the way to serve their neighbor—and through serving their neighbor to serve their God, and so fulfill themselves?

The vision of the Infinitely Great had been revealed to us through divine grace in the prison camp by the River Kwai. Now that we were back among the distractions and diversions of a materialistic world, we were determined to follow that vision.

In my conversations with other former P.O.W.'s, I found many who were thinking as I was. With tremendous urgency, they were seeking vocations where they could be of service to others.

As for myself, I thought at first I would return to the Far East, not, as I had pictured on the *Setia Berganti,* to be Adviser-in-Chief to the Sultan of Somewhere, but to engage in social work or to teach in Japan. These prospects, however, did not materialize.

I decided to follow the path along which I had been directed by my experiences in prison camps, and to study theology in preparation for the ministry.

In many ways it was not an easy choice to make, for it necessitated adjustment to an entirely different environment, language, and attitude. After my return I had gone to church every Sunday, but what I saw and heard depressed me. The sermons belonged to a different age. They suggested Victorian parlors, elderly people dressed in black, horsehair chairs and antimacassars. We had seen a vision of far horizons and caught a glimpse of the City of God in all its beauty.

I kept to my resolve and went for two years to theological college in Edinburgh. At the end of that time I received a fellowship at Hartford Theological Seminary in Connecticut. For two years I lived there with my wife while I was pursuing post-graduate studies in history.

My choice was not unusual among former P.O.W.'s. For years I kept hearing of other alumni of the hell camps who had gone into the ministry after having been in some other profession.

Among them was the Rev. Paul Miller, who is the vicar at Conor in Derbyshire, England. When he invited a Japanese from

Hiroshima, the Rev. John Kanoh, to be his curate, his parishioners resented the appointment, remembering the fate that their brothers, sons, and friends had suffered at the hands of the enemy.

Mr. Miller told his irate congregation,

"I want you to accept our newcomer as a member of the family."

Later on he said to reporters,

"It was grim being a prisoner on the Burma railroad, but I don't hold any bitterness for the Japanese. Their way of life is completely different. Japanese soldiers were severely punished by their own N.C.O.'s, so one would not expect them to treat prisoners with kindness.

"There are bound to be people in the village who won't like there being a Japanese curate. They will probably gossip about him in the pubs and clubs. I don't expect anyone to come directly to me and complain. The talking will be behind one's back. If any in the parish try to make things difficult for Father Kanoh, I shall visit them privately and give them a scolding—and it won't be so mild."

Many other P.O.W.'s chose their calling with the objective of serving their fellow man and contributing to the good of society. To this end, they became teachers, welfare officers, research technicians, or doctors. Among them was my friend John Leckie, who took up the study of medicine after he was "demobbed." The last time I heard from him, he was serving a coal-mining community in Wales, dispensing with his medicine a gentle pawky humor and a healing faith.

A fellow prisoner, John Perret, became interested in biology through his experience in camp when he learned to make medicines from the resources at hand. After the war he went to Cambridge and graduated with honors in science. Recently he demonstrated before the Royal Society a process whereby bacteria can be grown speedily and diluted at the same time that they are multiplying.

George Winston before the war was a sergeant in the regular artillery. Now, as vice-president of the Chemico Laboratories in Florida, he is working in the field of virus diseases. Recently he introduced a new drug, Reticulose, which he hopes will prove effective against virus-caused infections.

Sir Albert Coates, who did such brilliant work as a medical officer at Nakawm Paton, today is professor of surgery at Melbourne University. M. F. A. Woodruff, another M.O., is professor of surgery at Edinburgh University. Ronald Searle, famous cartoonist for *Punch, Holiday, Life,* and other magazines on both sides of the Atlantic, began his career by sketching both the horrors and the lighter side of life in the Southeast Asia prison camps.

Many human stories have come to my attention. At my daily company parade there was an Argyll who used to appear every Thursday morning as regular as clockwork, charged with some offense or other by the Red Caps. His conduct sheet was as long as one's arm. I didn't meet him again until some time later when I was at Paisley. He was looking prosperous and contented.

When we shook hands, the first words he said to me were,

"You'll not believe it—I'm never in trouble now."

He went on, with great pride, to tell me of his happy marriage, how he had started a little business which was succeeding very well, and how he was extremely active in community affairs.

"Do you go to church?" I asked.

"Och, aye," he answered to my astonishment. "And what's more, my name is up for the next lot of elders."

Another P.O.W., a fine, handsome man, was engaged to be married. He was the last surviving male of his family, his two brothers having been killed in action and his father in an air raid. He returned home to find his mother a chronic invalid and his sister tubercular from her service in the Auxiliary Territorial Service. The last I heard of him, he had given up all thoughts of marriage and was taking his mother and sister out to New Zealand where he would be better able to care for them.

Welfare and other charitable organizations have benefited from the zeal and enthusiasm of men like Stewart E. Bell, an Edinburgh advocate and an elder in St. Cuthbert's Church.

The list of extracurricular projects which former P.O.W.'s support is proof their interest in others has not flagged. They have helped build orphanages and hospitals and have supported welfare work in behalf of comrades and their dependents.

Associations of former P.O.W.'s sprang up all over Britain soon after our return. Now numbering seventy-nine, they have formed themselves into the Federation of Far Eastern Prisoners of War Clubs and Associations of Great Britain and Northern Ireland. The general aims of the F.E.P.O.W.'s are:

To promote the material and spiritual welfare of all F.E.P.O.W.'s and the dependents of those who died in captivity or subsequently, and to represent their interests by all legal means; to preserve the sacred memory of those who died in captivity or subsequently; to perpetuate the bonds of fellowship forged during captivity and to perpetuate the spirit that kept us all going during the years of imprisonment.

One of the objectives accomplished was to urge the government to seek compensation from the Japanese for the brutalities inflicted on us. This amounted to fifteen pounds, or forty-two dollars, for each of us. The sum was purely nominal; nevertheless, the principle had been established that never again should helpless P.O.W.'s be treated as the Japanese military had treated us.

When this motion was debated in the House, it was opposed by some M.P.'s on the ground that troops were expected to undergo such suffering. It was part of a soldier's pay.

Much more than financial help has been extended by former P.O.W.'s to one another. They have been unstinting in the giving of their time, energy, service, and counsel in every field of endeavor from housing to educational, religious, or family problems.

On the whole they appear to have made much more of a success of their lives in the difficult postwar period than those who had an easier time of it. This is borne out by a recent survey conducted by Dr. E. P. Routley, also a former P.O.W.

Dr. Routley found that more of them have married than in other comparable groups and that their marriages have been more lasting.

But statistics cannot tell us much of fears overcome, of aspirations realized, of the seeds of faith, hope, and love which lodged in their hearts to flower later in the lives of others.

I, too, sought an opportunity to put my experience to work. I had seen at first hand the cruelty of a totalitarian regime. I knew something of suffering and what it meant to look death in the face. I knew the depths to which men could sink and the heights to which they could rise. I could speak knowledgeably of despair, but also of hope; of hatred, but also of love; of man without God, but of man sustained by God. I knew the power of the demonic, and I knew the greater power of the Holy Spirit.

Many of the prisoners who had died in camp had been so young. I had felt their deaths keenly. I wanted ultimately to minister to the young, to those of college age. But I saw no way that my wish was to be achieved.

While I was still in the United States after I had completed my graduate studies at Hartford Theological Seminary, I told the executive secretary of the Board of Education of the Presbyterian Church about my interest in working with students. He suggested that I keep in touch with him. I returned to Scotland to do further work in history and to serve as assistant minister in the historic Abbey of Paisley. Three years elapsed. Then, at his urging, I resigned my post at the Abbey and returned to the United States.

I landed in New York without a charge or parish or definite prospect of any kind. I had my sympathetic wife, my children, and two hundred dollars to my name. Within a week I was invited to supply the Presbyterian churches of Amagansett and Montauk, neighboring villages at the eastern end of Long Island. Less than a year later I was in sight of the opportunity I had been seeking. I was called to be Presbyterian pastor at Princeton University. The following year I became Dean of the Chapel.

Here I found that although prison camp and campus were poles apart, many of the questions asked me were identical to those I had been called upon to answer in Southeast Asia. The miracle I knew in the jungle was being repeated daily on the campus—the miracle of God at work in His world.

I recalled that when I was at Paisley I had been told how the old-time weavers, all the while they were making their beautiful and intricate patterns, saw no more than the backs of their shawls. Nothing was visible to them but a tangle of colored threads. They never saw the design they were creating until they took the finished fabric from their looms.

The parallel to the mortal lot is plain. Human experience appears to us—as the shawls did to the weavers—to be no more than incomprehensible tangles of colored threads, whereas in fact life represents the ordered threads in a great design—the design being woven daily on the loom of eternity. Looking back, in all the chaos and confusion, I could see a splendid purpose being worked out.

In my time of decision, nature and reason were neutral. They did not speak to me of anything that made possible a significant understanding of myself and my fellow man. They did not show me the vision of the Infinitely Great.

Jesus, however, had spoken to me, had convinced me of the love of God, and had drawn me into a meaningful fellowship with other men as brothers. Because of him I had come to see the world in a new way as the creation of God—not purposeless but purposeful.

He had opened me to life and life to me.

In the prison camp we had discovered nothing new. The grace we had experienced is the same in every generation and must ever be received afresh.

The good news for man is that God, in Christ, has shared his suffering; for that is what God is like. He has not shunned the responsibility of freedom. He shares in the saddest and most painful experiences of His children, even that experience which seems to defeat us all, death itself.

He comes into our Death House to lead us through it.

Acknowledgments

I NEVER SERIOUSLY CONSIDERED WRITING A BOOK about my experience as a prisoner of war of the Japanese until it was suggested that I do so by Clarence W. Hall, senior editor of *The Reader's Digest*. This was the result of an interview he had with me which was published in the June, 1960, issue of the magazine as an article entitled "It Happened on the River Kwai." The response to the article was sufficient to indicate there might be a place for such a book. My reason for writing it is principally that it deals with the great issues of human experience which are never old, never dated. To live life in the personal dimension is to be involved with such issues. They are inescapable. All of us are on an Odyssey, for we are all wanderers, seeking a way. Those of us who were prisoners of the Japanese were very conscious of this truth.

I am grateful to the artists, Charles Thrale, Ronald Searle, Stanley Gimson, and Leo Rawlings, all former prisoners of the Japanese, for the privilege of reprinting their sketches.

I am grateful to those who have urged me to write this book; to my good friend Stewart E. Bell of Edinburgh for keeping me up-to-date on the careers of other former P.O.W.'s; to Mrs. Mathilde E. Finch for her kindness in reading the first draft, and to Edward R. Sammis for his patience and enthusiasm in his work as consulting editor.

E. G.